The
PACIFIC NORTHWEST

The
PACIFIC
NORTHWEST

MALLARD
PRESS

An Imprint of BDD Promotional Book Company
666 Fifth Avenue
New York, N.Y. 10103

MALLARD PRESS
An imprint of
BDD Promotional Book Company, Inc.
666 Fifth Avenue
New York, NY 10103

Mallard Press and its accompanying design and logo are
trademarks of BDD Promotional Book Company, Inc.

First published in the United States of America in 1990 by
Mallard Press.

Printed and Bound in Spain

ISBN 0-792-45094-9

Excerpts from *1989 Pacific Northwest* are reprinted with permission of
World of Travel Publishing, Inc., 106 South Front Street,
Philadelphia, PA 19106.

Producer: Solomon M. Skolnick
Designer: Ann-Louise Lipman
Editors: Terri L. Hardin, Madeline Larsen, Joan E. Ratajack
Production Coordinator: Valerie Zars
Picture Researcher: Edward Douglas
Editorial Assistant: Carol Raguso
Assistant Picture Researcher: Robert V. Hale

Title page: *To survive along the Oregon coast, vegetation must be hardy. Heavy rains and strong winds have been known to uproot even giant trees.* **Preceding pages:** *A view of Oregon's north coast from Ecola State Park, near Cannon Beach. Trails lead from the park to quiet coves which are popular picnic areas.*

LIFE AT THE CENTER

When I was growing up near Seattle, I used to travel once a year with my parents south on Highway 99 to attend the family reunion or, more rarely, to spend a day at Mount Rainier National Park. This was before there were freeways, when 99 was the main route out of town. South of the business district and the harbor, it passed through the industrial section, past the Boeing Aircraft Co., Isaacson Steel, and a cluster of low rocky hills covered with scrub vegetation and much scarred by development. They did not interest us as much as the nearby drive-in, built to look like a huge cowboy hat and flanked by two enormous boots, but that was because we were ignorant. We would have paid more attention had we realized that they marked the center of the world.

The center, at least, of the Duwamish world. The Duwamish were a Native American people that lived in the Seattle area for thousands of years before the first white settlers showed up in the 1850's. Anthropologists include them in a much larger grouping of native people called the Coast Salish. The Duwamish fished the Duwamish River, dug clams on nearby beaches, and hunted ducks in the marshes and deer in the forests. They spent the winter months in at least fifty villages made up of cedar-board longhouses and, when the world warmed, they broke into smaller groups in order to harvest Nature's bounty. When the salmon were migrating up the river, one of the places the Duwamish gathered to fish was at the cluster of low hills, the center of the world.

The hills flank the river at the site of its first rapids, where boulders trouble the waters and provide a good fishing station. One of the hills, a blunt promontory called Sbabadeel, "little mountain," is identified as the place where the "Four Ancients" came to make the primal division of the world. The hill was the center, the place of beginning, and the storied hills and rocks surrounding it commemorated events that marked the progress of the world's creation.

The rocks forming the rapids were said to be the remains of an ice fish weir which the frigid Northwind built across the river to keep the salmon from going upstream to spawn. Jealous of rivals, he killed the most powerful of them, his brother-in-law, the warm Southwind, and all of his enemy's people, save a old woman who fled to a hill where she wept for her murdered kinsmen. Eventually a hero, Stormwind, defeated Northwind with the help of this woman, who happened to be his grandmother and who had the power to bring spring rains. Together, these two figures, personifying the revivifying Chinook wind of spring and the floods that precede the salmon migration, destroyed the fish weir and restored warmth and life to the world. Northwind was driven out, and the remains of his fish weir, the grandmother, and several other supernatural beings that figure in the story were turned to stone, in a kind of Salish *Götterdammerung* at the end of the myth time.

I have made it part of my work as a writer to piece out these stories from a variety of fragmentary sources, in order to help the public become more aware of the rich cultural heritage they represent and the romance of the Northwestern landscape. As a result of years of public ignorance, none of these particular myth sites is in any way protected, and many are in danger of becoming more scarred than they already are. In spite of their cultural significance, they are not judged scenic enough to be preserved for esthetic purposes. Fortunately, not all sites suffer this debility.

Near the town of Northbend, 30 miles east of Seattle, Interstate 90 passes through the Snoqualmie Valley. It takes its name from the Snoqualmie people, another native group who also gave their name to the Snoqualmie River and its falls, which plunges a spectacular 268 feet over a cliff a few miles west of Northbend. Above the falls is a fertile prairie, won for the Snoqualmie, according to their legends, by their ancestors, the wolves, who won it from the grizzly bear people, its original possessors. The prairie is walled-in to the north by the imposing bulk of Mount Si, whose cliffs soar over 3,000 feet above it. To the south rises the long ridge of Rattlesnake Mountain, named by a pioneering survey party that mistook the rattling of seed pods for the sound of the snakes.

In the middle of the prairie there once rose a small rocky hill the Snoqualmie called Yidoad, "the swing," that was the central set piece on this grand stage for the legend of the star child, the heart of the Snoqualmie myth of creation. This told the story of two Snoqualmie sisters who were out digging fern roots on the prairie. Before they went to sleep under the starry sky, they imagined aloud about what it would be like to live in the star country. When they awoke, they found themselves among the star people, each beside a star husband.

They lived in the star country for a time, and one bore a son to her star husband, but eventually, they grew homesick. Once when they were out digging roots in the star prairie, they broke through to the sky below, and looking through the hole, they saw their village. They wove a long rope from cedar branches and climbed down carrying the star child, a boy who would one day grow up to become the moon.

The girls' parents rejoiced to have their daughters back with their wonder child, and the sisters taught their people how to swing on the hanging rope in a long, glorious arc from Rattlesnake Mountain clear to the top of Mount Si, a ride that took half a day. The canyons one can see shadowing the face of Rattlesnake Mountain in late afternoon are said to be the paths worn by the people's feet as they made a running start for the rope. Toward the end of the myth time, "Rat" gnawed the rope through and it fell to earth in a coiled heap, where it was later transformed into the hill Yidoad. In another version of the story, the rope became Snoqualmie Falls, forever falling from the prairie, a kind of primal Eden, to the lower valley where most of the Snoqualmie lived in historic times.

Yidoad was the mythic center of the Snoqualmie world, just as Sbabadeel was for the Duwamish. Every native group could point to features in their individual homelands that they honored similarly as places where nature and the supernatural worked together to empower and order the world. Some of these have been destroyed—quarried away like Yidoad to provide railroad ballast or rock for breakwaters—but others have been set aside in parks or protected areas, not because of their cultural importance, but because of their great beauty.

Mount Rainier, for example, is preserved in all its splendor in a national park. At 14,410 feet, it is the grandest of all the peaks in the Cascade Mountains, and it impressed the Native Americans no less than it does us today. It is the focus of numerous myths and legends that describe its supernatural character, and it is popularly known as "the mountain that was God." What is not generally known, however, is that it was actually a goddess whose name, although variously spelled, is most commonly rendered "Tahoma" or "Tacoma." Moreover, the goddess Tahoma was identified not as the whole mountain but rather as the smooth central cone of the peak, the central and highest point of its tridentate summit. The northernmost point, the prominence we call Liberty Cap, is identified as her grandson, the young hero who defends his grandmother from the cold north wind.

According to legend, Tahoma was the young wife of Koma Kulshan, the 10,778-foot peak near the Canadian border we call Mount Baker. He grew angry with her and drove her and her children from his house. They wandered south and came to rest where they are today, the great mountain standing in splendor, the minor peaks representing her children flanking the cone. She continues to wear her white bridal blanket, and the food plants she carried with her—roots, bulbs, and berries—grow abundantly in the meadows where she planted them.

What myths and legends like these reveal is that for the native people, the landscape had a supernatural, a spiritual dimension. Their homeland was also their holy land. Our capacity to appreciate the beauty of these landmarks and the folklore associated with them enables us to share in this unique perception of the natural environment. From the commanding heights of the great goddess Tahoma to the storied little hills south of Seattle, the center of the world, the Northwestern landscape emerges as a presence rich with character and meaning and with an enhanced claim on our affectionate regard. It is something those who love the land have always understood, for wherever the heart is, that is the center.

—David M. Buerge
Duwamish Tribal Historian

Elaborate walls, moats, and outbuildings are common additions to sand castle designs. Below: *Energetic artists create sculptured images in the sand during Cannon Beach's annual Sand Castle Day.*

Clamdiggers hunt for bay clams and razors at Seaside, where the warmest waters of the Pacific off the Oregon coast can be found. Below: *Big rocks off Chapman Point, also known as "seastacks," are common resting places for hundreds of gulls and other sea birds.*

Preceding page: *Ecola State Park's rugged cliffs, along with the battered trees and driftwood, give evidence of the storms this area has endured over time.* This page: *Haystack Rock off Cannon Beach is an imposing 235-foot monolith. The two vertical rocks are called "the Needles."*

A tidepool at Cannon Beach is home to small crabs, jellyfish, and other marine life that get swept in by the tides. Green slopes (left) lead down from Ecola State Park to Cannon Beach, in the distance, lush hills can be seen girding the coastline. Opposite: Although the waves crashing against the cliffs at Cape Kiwanda look treacherous, this is one of the few places in the world where boats are launched into the open surf from a sandy beach.

OREGON

The Oregon coast is, without question, the number-one tourist attraction in the Pacific Northwest. For 346 highway miles from Astoria, on the Columbia River, to the California border, the coast offers the most magnificent seascapes this side of Maine. Rocky coves, wave-battered headlands, long sandy beaches, tiny fishing ports, weathered small towns, elegant resorts, wind-sculpted woodlands, offshore sea stacks— all combine to give the coast a unique, multifaceted personality.

The coast is accessible. Except for a few miles, U.S. 101 hugs the shoreline all the way. A foresighted governor in 1912 declared all but 21 miles of the coast a public highway. In the 1960's, the Oregon legislature preserved the beaches for "free and uninterrupted use" by the public. Thus, development is kept off the beach and the scenic shoreline preserved for the enjoyment of all.

The north coast is historic, dotted with small towns and modest-but-comfortable inns, hotels, and motels. The central coast, around Lincoln City and Newport, is the most developed. The south coast, except for the area around Coos Bay, is wild and primitive, with small towns scattered at wide intervals.

Winter storm watching has created a whole new season for visitors, and in late spring, you get the bonus of dazzling displays of rhododendrons and azaleas as well as Scotch broom brightening the landscape.

Along about November, the first big storm comes roaring out of the Gulf of Alaska to slam against the North Pacific coast with gale-force winds and thundering waves. When the barometer starts plummeting and the weatherman announces a storm on the way, many inland city dwellers bundle into the car and head for the coast.

There's a technique to storm watching. First, you must select a place on the coast where you have a good view of the action. Ideally, you should have a fireplace and plenty of wood to keep a cozy fire going. Stock a good supply of your favorite food and wine. To cap it all off, bring along a tape or CD player and a supply of music appropriate to storm watching—Wagner, for instance. Then, settle back and listen to the howl of the wind in the eaves and watch while waves try to batter the rocks to smithereens.

Typically, these storms don't last more than a couple of days and there are generally lulls (when it will probably be raining) in between bursts of fury. That's when you put on your heavy woolens, top them off with rain gear and go beachcombing. These winter storms toss all manner of flotsam and jetsam up on the beach—contorted pieces of driftwood good for decorating, parts of packing crates and other wooden objects from passing ships. Those who are very lucky come away with one of those treasures all beachcombers prize, a green or gray Japanese glass fishing float. The waves also uncover beautiful stones and shells.

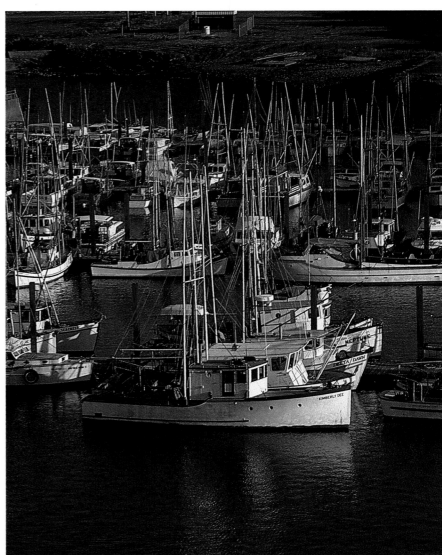

Preceding page, clockwise from left: *Fishing fleets ride at anchor at Yaquina Bay at Newport, Oregon, which has extensive public moorage and jetties for both sport and commercial fishermen. Rock-bound Depot Bay, Oregon, is a popular berthing place for many deep-sea trawlers; during the summer season, the boats fish offshore for salmon, red snapper, and other fish. A delicate-looking iron bridge spans Yaquina Bay at Newport on the Oregon coast.* This page: *Agate Beach near Newport, with Yaquina Lighthouse in the background. The light station's tower stands 96 feet tall, making it the highest of all coastal lighthouses. Agate Beach is one of the finest agate-hunting sites in the world. Fossils can also be found here, on an outgoing tide.*

Among Oregon's most recognizable natural wonders is Crater Lake. The lake is the deepest (and the most incredibly blue) in North America, 1,932 feet deep, six miles long, with a 20-mile shoreline. The crater in which it lies is what remains of 12,000-foot Mount Mazama, which erupted almost 7,000 years ago. Sheer cliffs rise 2,000 feet above the lake.

It is clear from archeological evidence that early people witnessed (and were in some cases the victims of) the explosion. Artifacts, including 75 pairs of charred sandals (dating back to the time of the cataclysm), were unearthed at Fort Rock, 70 miles from the north rim of the crater. Many stories about the eruption of Mount Mazama and the creation of Crater Lake entered into local mythology. Descendants of Native Americans considered the area taboo well into the nineteenth century.

The Cascade Range, much of it over 10,000 feet in elevation, separates Oregon and Washington into two distinct subregions, where climate, economics, demographics and social structure are quite different, depending on whether you're east or west of the mountains.

Within just a few miles on either side of the Hood River, weather and terrain change dramatically. To the west, rain clouds often hover just above the lofty basalt cliffs, foliage is lush green, and water is abundant. To the east, the land is semidesert, and dry brown hills are capped with waving prairie grass, wheat fields or sage brush; days are mostly sunny and the weather, in summer, is hot.

The climate near Mount Hood is good for tree fruit and wine grapes. As you climb through the orchards on Oregon 35, the near-perfect snow-capped cone of 11,235-foot Mount Hood appears and disappears close at hand. Within a few miles, you lose sight of the mountain and plunge into thick conifer forests, continuing to climb along the East Fork of Hood River around the mountains shoulder.

Mount Hood is a superb mountain recreation area offering winter sports, and hiking, climbing, camping and fishing in summer. Mount Hood is not considered a difficult climb and thousands of people reach the summit, guided and equipped by professionals from Government Camp, each year.

The reason most visitors from out of state come to Mount Hood is not the skiing or summer hiking, but Timberline Lodge. One of the great architectural masterpieces of the West, Timberline was a make-work project of the WPA in the 1930's. Hundreds of skilled (and unemployed) artisans—stonemasons, woodcarvers, sculptors, ironworkers, coppersmiths, weavers, painters and muralists—were put to work creating this massive lodge that stands on the south slope of the mountain. From the huge iron door hinges to the three-story stone fireplace in

Preceding page: *The Heceta Head Lighthouse, just south of Newport. This page, top to bottom: Oregon's coastline offers miles of some of the largest and oddest offshore rock formations. The most dramatic is Devil's Punch Bowl, near Otter Rock. During the summer months, the mating season of the silver smelt, thousands of these little fish travel to the sandy coves of Yachats, Oregon and People come from miles around to catch them, using special nets.*

The coastal dunes, part of the Oregon Band Dunes National Recreation Area, are changeable and mysterious. Conservationists plant beach grass and broom to try to stabilize the area. Below: Covering over 32,000 acres, the dunes rise to heights of more than 250 feet. Countless lakes and pools are also scattered throughout this area, but many of them dry up in late summer.

the soaring lobby, everything is crafted by hand. Furniture, lamps, wall hangings, the newel posts on the stairs that are carved into bears and owls—it's all one great craft museum that is preserved on the register of historic places. The lodge has magnificent views south to Mount Jefferson, Broken Top, and the Three Sisters.

Mount Hood National Forest provides plenty of opportunity to get out in the woods within easy reach (about 50 miles) of Portland. For hiking in a natural setting there are the Mount Hood, Salmon-Huckberry, Columbia, Badger Creek, and Bull of the Woods wildernesses. All are laced with well-maintained trails and primitive campsites. Lost Lake, on the north side of the mountain, has calm waters and unique mirror-image views of Mount Hood.

Shore Acres State Park, near Coos Bay. Below: *Large vessels are a common sight in Coos Bay. Lumber, a major industry, is shipped from here.* Overleaf, page left: *Boardman State Park, on the southern Oregon coast.* Overleaf, page right: *Bandon Beach, Oregon.*

Preceding pages: *Sunset at Bandon Beach, Oregon.* This page: *Two views of Bandon Beach.* Page right: *A field of bright yellow skunk cabbage (top) near southern Oregon's Cape Blanco, so named because of its chalk-white cliffs. Spectacular Cannon Beach (bottom).*

Two things strike visitors to Portland before they've been in the city very long—its small-town flavor and its real-life people scale.

Portland is often compared to a favorite aunt, a bit dowdy, but loving and comfortable to be around. With a population of 366,400 and a metropolitan population exceeding 1.3 million, Portland is hardly small. Yet, it has also been called "the biggest small town in the West," because it feels that way.

The city's downtown core is easy to get around on foot. More importantly, it doesn't overwhelm you as many eastern cities do. The tallest building in town is only 40 stories high. And, the city's planners had the forethought to devote lots of space to parks and open areas; there's greenery nearly everywhere you turn. Vigorous preservation efforts have saved much of Portland's nineteenth-century architecture, so the new high-rises that are beginning to dominate the horizon are tempered and softened by many handsome, smaller buildings.

Portland was founded by New Englanders and named for Portland, Maine. The story goes that A.J. Lovejoy of Boston and Francis Pettygrove of Portland, Maine, surveyed a town site of 16 blocks on the west bank of the Willamette River in 1844. Each wanted to name it for his hometown. They decided by the toss of a coin.

Preceding pages: *Cradled in the shattered crest of Mount Mazama, which erupted over 6,000 years ago, is Crater Lake.* This page and opposite: *Crater Lake and its two islands: Wizard Island (top), which rises about 760 feet above the surface of the lake; and Phantom Ship (opposite), the smaller of the islands.*

John Day Fossil Beds National Monument, central Oregon. At the arid Painted Hills, tiny seashells, teeth, and bones dating back over 40 million years can be found. Below: *The John Day River flows past the base of Sheep Rock.* Opposite: *Gray, green, and brown tones are visible in this area, which was once covered by an ancient sea.* Overleaf: *Mirror Lake in the Three Sisters range of the Cascade Mountains. Lava fields and stands of hemlock and fir surround the area.*

Preceding page: *Proxy Falls, a veil of water that drops 200 feet onto moss-covered rocks and logs in the Three Sisters Wilderness area.* This page: *The Three Sisters, which rise to heights above 10,000 feet, have more than 240 miles of trails. They remain covered in snow long after the lower regions have experienced the blossoms of spring.* Overleaf: *South Sister, as viewed from the top of Middle Sister. A glacial lake sits in the lower region, while Mount Bachelor appears over the mountain's left shoulder.*

Mount Jefferson, over 10,000 feet high, lies to the west of the Three Sisters and is considered by many to be a hiker's paradise.

Mount Bachelor, known for its challenging alpine ski runs, towers over Lake Todd, which reflects the clouds overhead. Overleaf: A chain of volcanos viewed from Middle Sister. From left to right, Mount Washington, Three Fingered Jack, Mount St. Helens, Mount Jefferson, Mount Hood, and Mount Adams.

The hundreds of immigrants crossing the continent on the Oregon Trail in the 1840's were headed for the Willamette Valley; but the light at the end of the tunnel, so to speak, was Portland. Most of them floated down the Columbia from The Dalles in canoes, rafts, boats, or anything that would float; some came overland around Mount Hood. But after months of slogging across prairie, desert and mountain, the rain-soaked shacks standing in a mud wallow beside the Willamette probably looked like paradise.

The California Gold Rush, which came along in the 1850's, meant early prosperity for Portland. Many overland immigrants chose the easier route to California via the Oregon Trail and passed through Portland. Timber and other products for the California gold fields were shipped from the busy river ports.

Today, Portland thrives primarily because of its port, the third largest on the West Coast. Timber and grain are outbound; containers full of all kinds of goods for shipment east are inbound.

Portland's western hills have some of the loveliest residential sections of any city in the country. Portlanders are avid gardeners (it is called "the Rose City"), so their landscaping tends to be superb.

Council Crest Park is the highest point in the city (1,073 feet) and has sweeping views north and east to the snow-capped ridges of the Cascades.

Several of Portland's most popular attractions are clustered in 145-acre Washington Park. The Portland Zoo is one: outstanding among zoos, it has gained a worldwide reputation in recent years for the successful breeding of elephants in captivity (more than 20 born since 1962). In addition to the routine zoo animals, this zoo has an Alaska Tundra exhibit and a Cascades exhibit where you can view flora and fauna native to the Pacific Northwest. The zoo train is pulled by a working steam engine on summer weekends; at other times a diesel pulls you along a four-mile track through the woods. In the summer, the zoo hosts jazz and bluegrass concerts.

OMSI (Oregon Museum of Science and Industry, pronounced by Portlanders "ahm-see"), is across from the zoo and houses an extensive collection of hands-on science and nature exhibits, from working beehives and chick hatcheries to electricity demonstrations and a Foucault Pendulum.

Nearby, the World Forestry Center has lumber industry exhibits. Tetra I, operated by the local electric utility, is an experimental energy-efficient house.

The park's International Rose Test Gardens display more than 4,000 rose bushes (400 varieties) on four-and-a-half acres, a brilliant show of blossoms during Rose Festival week in June. Another five-and-a-half acres is devoted to the precisely landscaped Japanese Garden. The zoo train has special stops for these gardens.

Built during the Depression, Mount Hood's Timberline Lodge is a rustic masterpiece of stone, timber, and ironwork. **Right:** *Rising over 11,000 feet, Mount Hood is the highest point in Oregon. About 90 miles from Portland, its slopes are a popular playground for skiers and hikers.* **Opposite:** *A view of Mount Hood from Timberline Lodge.*

Hood River Valley. During the spring, the fruit trees are awash with white and pink blossoms. Below: The trees will later bear apples, pears, and cherries. Opposite: Mount Hood and the Cascade range can be seen rising over the east side of Portland, the state's largest city.

Proud of its pioneer heritage and its links to the Wild West, Portland remembers its past and celebrates its present. Below: The "Portland" sign marks the city's Center for the Performing Arts complex, three theaters that are used for live music and theatrical performances. Opposite: The Civic Auditorium; in the foreground is "The People's Fountain," a series of waterfalls that splash over concrete blocks into sparkling pools.

First Congregational Church (1891) in the Park Blocks district. Early settlers set this area of Portland aside to protect it from commercial construction. **Right:** *A statue of Sacajawea in Portland's Washington Park. Sacajawea was the Indian guide who helped explorers Lewis and Clark find the overland route to Oregon.* **Below:** *The Manor is one of many fine buildings on the campus of Lewis and Clark College in Portland.*

In a lovely setting with snow-capped Mount Hood and jagged-topped Mount St. Helens on the horizon, Portland straddles the Willamette River. It's a delight for bridge fanciers. 11 spans—St. John's, Five Point One, Fremont, Broadway, Steel, Burnside, Morrison, Hawthorne, Marquam, Ross Island, Sellwood—tie the two halves of the city together and no two are alike. At one time each was even painted a different color.

Portland's two historic districts—Yamhill and Old Town— lie just across Front Avenue within four blocks of each other. Experts have identified these two districts as containing the finest remaining examples of cast-iron architecture in the country. As you stroll the old streets, look upward occasionally and you'll see ornate scrollwork, filigree, animal and human figures, and other building details, all cast in iron.

Highlights of the area include Yamhill Marketplace (a farmer's market with bakeries and food concessionaires), the 1879 Bishop's House, the 1886 Henry Failing Building, the New Market Theater Block, the Bickel Building, Smith's Block, the Glisan Building, Merchant's Hotel, and Erickson's Saloon. During the summer months you can ride through the districts in a horse-drawn carriage from in front of Skidmore Fountain. The American Advertising Museum, Oregon Historic League, and Oregon Maritime Center and Museum are also located in the historic district.

Typical of Oregon's maverick character is the Saturday Market. On Saturdays and Sundays, from April through Christmas, an eclectic conglomeration of food vendors, artisans and craftsmen, musicians, jugglers, magicians, storytellers, and you-name-it gathers beside the Burnside Bridge to dispense their wares and entertain.

First-time visitors to the Willamette Valley often remark that it looks a lot like parts of New England, especially the small towns. That's because it was settled by New Englanders.

Others are sure it looks more like the Midwest of Ohio, Illinois, and Indiana. That's because it was also settled by Midwesterners.

American history in the Far West begins in the Willamette Valley. Here, in 1843, Oregon pioneers formed the provisional government for the first American commonwealth on the Pacific Coast. Newberg, settled by Quakers, was home to Herbert Hoover as a child, though he was born in Iowa. The Minthorn House, his boyhood home, is operated as a museum.

Today, the Willamette Valley is covered-bridge country—another legacy of the New England and Midwestern pioneers who settled the area. The state has 53 of them; most are still in use, but some were preserved and set aside when roads were widened or rerouted.

They're romantic anachronisms, reminders of a time when life was simpler, slower. Despite that they were once known as "kissing bridges (they were favorite spots for 'spooning')," covered bridges were built that way for very practical reasons. Covering the bridge timbers sheltered them from Oregon's frequent rains and extended their life as much as double or triple that of the normal, uncovered span. And though they look as if they were built in the nineteenth century, most were built in the 1920's and 1930's. The oldest was built in 1914; the youngest (not counting rebuilds) in 1947.

Seven bridges are clustered along streams just east of Albany—Bohemian Hall (1947), Gilkey (1939), Hannah (1936), Hoffman (1936), Larwood (1939), Shimanek (1966), and Weddle (1937).

❧ ❧ ❧

Around the time of the last Ice Age, tremendous floes of ice and water sliced through the volcanic rock of the Cascade Range, carving an enormous gorge and a route for the waters of the Columbia River to reach the sea. The result is a natural wonder that is awesome in its beauty. For more than 50 miles, 400-foot sheer cliffs bracket the river on either side. Waterfalls plunge from the rim and cascade into the gorge in mist and spray. On most days, rainbows arc over the falls and sometimes all the way over the gorge itself.

The Columbia continues to capture the imagination of those who traveled on it or beside it, just as it did in 1805 when Meriwether Lewis and William Clark descended the Columbia in canoes, following the "Great River of the West" to the glorious Pacific.

In Salem, the stark-white Capitol is topped by a gilt statue, the Golden Pioneer. This marble sculpture commemorates the Lewis and Clark expedition of 1804-1806. Center: *The fountain at Tom McCall Waterfront Park on the edge of the Willamette River. Portland residents can now rest, play, and dine in an area that was once an industrial wasteland.* Bottom: *"Portlandia," nearly as large as the Statue of Liberty, is in front of the Portland Building, the city's new center for city services.*

The Hot Air Balloon Classic is just one of many special activities that takes place during Portland's annual Rose Festival. Below: *Situated on 46 acres of land, the Pittock Mansion is a fine example of French Renaissance architecture. Built in 1914 by the founder of* The Oregonian, *it is now open to the public.* Opposite: *In the heart of Portland's Washington Park, stone lanterns, weeping willows, cherry trees, and quiet streams lend their beauty to the Japanese Gardens.*

Visible for miles along the Columbia River Gorge, Beacon Rock stands 848 feet tall, with trails composed of ramps, steps, and bridges leading to the top. Below: *Vista House, high above the Columbia River Gorge at Crown Point.*

Two spectacular waterfalls at the Columbia River Gorge: Upper McCord Creek Falls, at 125 feet (top), and Multnomah Falls (bottom), the highest waterfall in Oregon, at 620 feet.

Preceding pages, left: *Silver Falls State Park abounds with waterfalls; the highest, at 177 feet, is South Falls.* Preceding pages, right: *An osprey nest atop old pilings. Ospreys feed on inshore fish like those found in the Columbia River.* This page: *The lower Columbia at Longview, Washington. The Cascade Mountains (top) sit east of the river with Mount St. Helens rising in the background. Northhead Lighthouse (bottom) at the mouth of the Columbia River.*

WASHINGTON

On a quiet Sunday morning, May 18, 1980, Mount St. Helens erupted in a tremendous explosion that made headlines (and carried ash) around the world. Within seconds, 1,277 feet of the mountaintop vaporized in a billowing cloud of steam and ash. The eruption lasted nine hours and had a force equal to 400 million tons of TNT. Four billion cubic yards of mountain were displaced, enough to provide one ton of ash for every person on earth. The timber downed came to 3.2 billion board feet. At least 57 lives were lost.

The volcano is dormant now and you can even, if you wish, get permission to climb its snow-clad flanks. The easiest place to view Mount St. Helens is from the visitor's center at Castle Rock. Outside, if the weather is clear, you can view the crater through telescopes.

The 14,410-foot bulk of Mount Rainier dominates the horizon from almost anywhere in the Puget Sound region. The tallest volcanic mountain in the "lower 48 states," Mount Rainier was once 16,000 feet high. However, the 26 glaciers on and around Rainier (comprising the largest glacier system in the continental U.S.) have worn 2,000 feet away during the past 75,000 years. Particularly dramatic, glacier-clad and sparkling in the sunlight, Rainier rises almost two miles above the forested foothills with no other major mountain near it to compete for visual attention.

Running like a spine down the western third of the state, the Cascade Mountains effectively divide Washington into a wet side and a dry side. Most of the population, industry and rainfall lies west of the Cascades; the eastern two-thirds of the state is sparsely populated, relatively dry, and mostly devoted to agriculture. These mountains (Rainier being the highest) are relatively young and quite rugged. They're punctuated by five volcanoes—Mount Baker (10,778 feet), Glacier Peak (10,541), Rainier (14,410), Mount Adams (12,307 feet), and Mount St. Helens (once 9,677 feet; now 8,364).

❧ ❧ ❧

The big green-and-white Washington State ferry threads its way through narrow saltwater channels, twisting and turning past rocky points where evergreens grow right down to the water's edge, tiny coves dotted with sailboats, and beaches strewn with driftwood. From windows in the passenger lounge you can watch tugs towing log rafts, jaunty commercial fishing boats, and perhaps a pod of frolicsome killer whales.

When the ferry noses in to an island dock, people crowd forward to watch a parade of automobiles, delivery trucks, and bicycles clank over the steel ramp and disappear up a country road.

The 172-island archipelago (which grows to 450 islands at low tide) lies scattered over 179 square miles at the eastern approaches to the Strait of Juan de Fuca and within sight of Canada. Places of incomparable beauty, these islands are quiet, bucolic, and relatively isolated. Only about 10 of the islands are inhabited (year-round population: 9,000); automobile ferries stop at four of them.

The San Juans are sublime. Their slow pace provides the ideal retreat from urban life in the fast track. The San Juans are reminiscent of parts of New England—small fishing fleets in snug harbors, subsistence farms carved from the evergreen forest, and quiet settlements studded with clapboard and shingle-sided buildings. Like New England, the islands are home to dozens of well-known authors and artists. The locals respect their privacy and don't talk about them much, but you may rub elbows with a best-selling author in a country store and never recognize him or her. The islands are a favorite destination for boaters who come to take advantage of the protected waters, secluded island harbors, and relatively short distance from marinas at Seattle, Everett, and Anacortes.

❧ ❧ ❧

Lopez is the first island ferry stop, about 45 minutes from Anacortes. Quiet country roads meander down the island past flocks of fat sheep grazing in shoulder-high grass. Spur roads lead to the water's edge at several bays and beaches ideal for strolling or spreading a picnic lunch. Odlin County Park and Spencer Spit State Park, at the northern end of the island, have camping facilities with lovely marine views. For picnicking or beachcombing, Agate Beach, on the southwest side, is ideal.

Orcas Island, largest of the San Juans (57 square miles) and shaped like a horseshoe, is rolling, hilly, and heavily forested, rising to summits of 1,500 and 2,409 feet along the west and east legs. Stiff grades and shoulderless roads make it difficult for bicycling, but you can rent mopeds for leisurely exploring. Secluded coves, gravel beaches, and tree-fringed bluffs line 125 miles of shoreline, where low tides expose tidepools alive with tiny crabs, spiny anemones, and other saltwater denizens.

Marine wildlife is one of the primary reasons Pacific Northwesterners come to these islands. With patience and a good pair of binoculars, you're likely to spot resident bald eagles, river otters, and a passing parade of porpoises, orcas (killer whales), and minke whales.

Eastsound, at the apex of the horseshoe, is the business center and largest community, but it's a cozy, casual sort of place that invites you to explore on foot, poking into stores, cafés, galleries, and the museum at your leisure.

Eastsound dates from the 1880's. Several buildings remain from that period, including the beautiful little Emmanuel Episcopal Church (c. 1886) and the Outlook Inn (c. 1883). A cluster of six venerable log cabins contains the Orcas Historical Museum, featuring pioneer and Native American artifacts. The little village comes alive on Saturdays, from April to October, when local vendors and craftspeople sell everything from organic produce and flowers to ceramics and watercolors at the farmer's market on the museum grounds. A massive, rusted iron whale sculpture identifies Orcas Center, location of a 230-seat community theater that schedules plays, concerts, jazz, and classical performances throughout the year.

Rosario Resort, on the eastern side of the island, is a destination in itself. Built as an estate in 1904 by Robert Moran, a Seattle mayor and shipbuilding tycoon, it is lavish. The mansion boasts parquet floors, rare hardwood paneling, stained glass, and lots of comfort. The current owners periodically give public concerts on the 1,972-pipe organ that dominates the music room.

Preceding pages: *Mount St. Helens blew its top in a volcanic eruption in 1980, losing 1,300 feet of its cone and turning the verdant countryside into a "moonscape."* **This page:** *The fertile Lewis River Valley in the Gifford Pinchot National Forest lies just southeast of Mount St. Helens. Lava beds, mineral springs, and lakes can also be found in this area.* **Opposite:** *Steam rises from Mount St. Helens' crater.*

Mount Rainier, Washington's most celebrated and highest mountain at 14,410 feet.

Mount Adams, due east of the steaming Mount St. Helens, pierces the clouds at more than 12,000 feet above sea level. Below: An abandoned farmhouse, with Mount Adams in the distance. Opposite: Oregon's Mount Hood overlooks Lost Lake. Snow-covered for much of the year, skiing often continues on the mountain's upper slopes well into July.

Snoqualmie Falls, in Washington's Cascade Mountains (left) and (below) Image Lake at Tenpeak Mountain, a refreshing sight to hikers in the high country.

Part of the old Moran estate is now Moran State Park, 5,000 acres of pristine beaches, rocky headlands, freshwater lakes, and a dense forest of fir, hemlock, and cedar.

The sunset views from the top of Mount Constitution are absolutely stunning. The San Juan Islands lie scattered at your feet; to the east, snow-mantled 10,778-foot Mount Baker and the Cascades punctuate the skyline; to the west and south you can see Vancouver Island and the snowy bulk of the Olympic Mountains.

✄ ✄ ✄

San Juan Island is distinctly different from either Lopez or Orcas. Rows of commercial fishing boats and pleasure craft lie snugged into berths. The main street of Friday Harbor rises gently into town, flanked by weathered clapboard buildings.

San Juan Island is nearly as large as Orcas and the most populous of the islands. Friday Harbor, a metropolis by island standards (population 1,200), is the county seat of San Juan County. The Whale Museum is just uphill from the ferry landing. Devoted to the orca or killer whale native to these waters, displays explain that "killer" is a misnomer for these gentle mammals who only prey on fish. There are special exhibits for children, recordings of whale sounds, and a whale hotline over which the latest whale sightings are phoned in and posted on a map. Sighting and getting close to a pod of killer whales is a thrilling experience.

One of American history's comic events – the Pig War – took place on San Juan Island. In 1859, England and the United States both claimed the San Juan Islands. The situation came to a head that year when a pig belonging to Charles J. Griffin, an Englishman, raided a vegetable garden belonging to Lyman A. Cutler, an American. Cutler shot the pig. Troops from both countries, dispatched to the island to protect their citizens, built fortifications and postured a lot, but nobody started shooting. After several months, the garrisons settled down to an exchange of parties and banquets between camps until Kaiser Wilhelm I of Germany, arbitrating the dispute, awarded the San Juans to the United States in 1872.

San Juan Island National Historical Park now encompasses both sites. English Camp, 10 miles north of Friday Harbor at Garrison Bay, preserves the original barracks, guardhouse, hospital, and commissary. American Camp, on the southeastern tip of the island, has two original buildings and a self-guiding interpretive trail.

The Hotel De Haro, the island's primary resort, is also one of its historic treasures. Built in 1886 around a former Hudson's Bay Company fur trading post, the hotel originally housed visitors and business clients of a large lime and cement operation at Roche Harbor.

Inside, the small lobby looks much as it did in 1906 when Teddy Roosevelt stayed here. A five-foot-tall photo of the president hangs near the front desk over a register with his signature. The 122 rooms upstairs are furnished with period antiques.

San Juan Island is a great place to watch wildlife. Numerous bald eagles, golden eagles, and great horned owls feed on a large rabbit population and the abundant fish just offshore. Lime Kiln Lighthouse, on the west side of the island, is in the first whale-watching park in the country.

Above: *Just south of the Canadian border, many of Mount Shuksan's jagged peaks and glaciers remain snow-covered virtually year-round.* Below: *The rocky peaks of Mount Index in the Cascades.* Overleaf: *Hidden Lake, one of the smaller bodies of water in the North Cascades National Park region.*

Like most youngsters, Seattle hasn't quite made up its mind what it wants to be. Once a collection of shacks huddled on the mud flats of Elliott Bay in the 1850's, today it has a downtown full of high-rises and a very cosmopolitan outlook. But beneath the makeup, much of Seattle is still the small-town kid, a bit uncomfortable about being pushed toward center stage.

The city's first big break came with the discovery of gold in Canada's Klondike in 1897. On July 17, the steamer *Portland* arrived at Seattle's waterfront with a ton of gold aboard, and the rush was on. Within weeks, the sleepy little lumber town was transformed into a roisterous, brawling, jam-packed, supercharged port city, outfitting Klondike-bound prospectors. Paved streets, trolleys, five-and six-story buildings, hotels, restaurants, and a fleet of steamships dragged the City-by-the-Sound into the twentieth century, never to look back.

The second great leap took place in 1962. True, Seattle had grown in size and importance as the major financial and supply center for Alaska, as a lumber and fishing port and rail center, and as the funnel through which hundreds of thousands of members of the Armed Forces passed on their way overseas during World War II. But it remained, as one newspaper columnist insisted, "that rainy village between San Francisco and Alaska."

On Friday, April 20, 1962, Emmett Watson, then a columnist for the *Seattle Post-Intelligencer,* wrote, "Five o'clock on Friday would be as good a time as any. Five o'clock would be a good time—if only in your mind's eye—to take a long, last look around Seattle as you know it—to reflect, perhaps, or think hard on this city and what is happening to it. Seattle will never be the same again... Even now, I think, few among us really comprehend how the Fair is going to change the tempo, the outlook and the character of this city."

Preceding page top: *During the warmer summer months, little snow is left on Prusik Peak in the North Cascades, except for icy patches floating on the clear, cold Enchantment Lakes.* Bottom: *Patches of snow dot the rocky ridges that encircle deep, dark Doubtful Lake in North Cascades National Park.* This page: *Two views of Mount Baker, located near the Canadian border in the North Cascades. American Indians native to the region called Mount Baker "the Great White Watcher."*

The next morning the gates of Century 21, the Seattle World's Fair, swung wide. The audacity of a handful of civic leaders had created the first postwar U.S. fair and the first of the "jewelbox" world's fairs. Most of Seattle was a bit surprised by the whole thing. The fair created an atmosphere of change for the following decades that brought Seattle such things as liquor on Sundays, world-class performing arts, restaurants that served something besides steak or salmon, bed-and-breakfast inns, super ferries, waterfront streetcars, winter boat service to Victoria, major league sports, and the Kingdome.

Sophisticated travelers view Seattle as a new "in" destination. And Seattle is responding by providing a more sophisticated city for them to visit.

The reasons are many. Rand McNally's naming the city the number-one vacation destination in America in 1986 didn't hurt. As the closest gateway to the Orient, the city is being discovered by thousands of travelers on their way to and from somewhere else. Food writers are lavishing praise on Seattle restaurants and Northwest cuisine. The state's wineries and micro-breweries are gaining attention. And, perhaps most important of all, the city and its environs offer a fresh, new urban vacation setting of clean air and water, magnificent views (when it's not raining), and a tree-clad outdoors waiting to be explored. In no other U.S. city does the outdoors—forest, mountains, water—play such an important part in the lifestyles of its residents as well as the experiences of visitors.

Fruit orchards in the Wenatchee Valley in the East Cascades become a sea of white and pink blossoms in springtime. **Below:** *With the autumn freezes, deciduous plants in the Wenatchee National Forest produce red, gold, and bleached-white leaves.* **Opposite:** *The lush greens of summer surround this high-country stream in the Cascade Mountains.*

Rocky beaches and secluded coves make up much of Washington's San Juan Islands. 42 islands are undeveloped and open to campers who can get there by boat. Below: Sunset over Rosario Strait in the San Juan Islands. Opposite: The Lime Kiln Lighthouse and the English Camp date (top) back to 1860; they are now part of the San Juan Island National Historical Park. The historic Hotel De Haro at Roche Harbor (bottom) on the north end of San Juan Island.

Seattle is nearly surrounded by water. Puget Sound, an arm of the Pacific Ocean (which is 90 air-miles west), brackets the city to the west; 27-mile-long freshwater Lake Washington flanks it to the east. The Lake Washington Ship Canal connects fresh and salt water at the Hiram Chittenden Locks in the northwest part of the city.

In between, business and residential districts are squeezed into a narrow neck of land punctuated by six hills. First-time visitors are often surprised to find downtown streets hilly like those of San Francisco (and requiring the same driving skills.) In general, streets run east and west; avenues north and south.

Getting around is easy, and most of the attractions are best experienced on foot. Central business district buses are free and the Monorail speeds quickly between downtown (5th and Stewart) and the Seattle Center.

From the observation deck of the 605-foot Space Needle you have a 360-degree view of the city and Puget Sound, backdropped by the snow-capped Cascade range to the east and the Olympic Mountains to the west. An illustrated locator adjacent to the windows defines major landmarks and helps you get your bearings.

If the day is clear, you may hear Seattleites verify it with the remark, "The mountain's out." No one ever specifies which mountain, but it's Mount Rainier that dominates the south-eastern skyline.

Rich agricultural land in Washington's Skagit Valley provides many of the tulips and daffodils sold throughout the country. During the spring, miles of flat fields explode in colors of red, white, and yellow. **Opposite:** *Logs are grouped together in Everett's port for eventual transport and processing.*

Spread at the foot of the Space Needle, Seattle Center, the 74-acre legacy of the 1962 World's Fair, is the city's cultural heart. The acres of lawns, trees, fountains, and plazas provide a green oasis in any season, but on weekends and fair-weather days between April and October, it's a beehive of activity with outdoor concerts, amusement park attractions, impromptu performances, and special events.

The multi-building Pacific Science Center, its lacy arches towering above reflecting pools, is the genius of famed architect Minoru Yamasaki. Inside is an IMAX theater that exhibits science and nature films, a replica of a Northwest Indian longhouse, a hands-on mathematics and physics area that delights children, a star show and models of spacecraft, and a Lasarium.

On the north and west sides of the complex, you'll find the Coliseum (home of the NBA SuperSonics, rock concerts, and trade shows), the 3,100-seat Opera House, the 890-seat Bagley Wright Theater, and the Arena.

If the Seattle Center is the city's heart, then the Pike Place Market is its soul. One of the last authentic farmer's markets in the country, Pike Place was founded in 1907 and has grown higgledy-piggledy into a three-story rabbit warren of fish and meat markets, spice shops, vegetable vendors, delicatessens, craft shops, secondhand stores, and several restaurants. Shops have also spread across the street to neighboring Sanitary Market and beyond.

It seems incredible now that anyone could even think of tearing down this wonderful, funky, very human sort of place.

The Space Needle at night, with strong colors and high voltage, resembles a space craft hovering over the city. **Opposite:** *This statue of Chief Seattle (top, right) is on the grounds of the Seattle Center, although there are many statues of the great man throughout the city. This modern sculpture and the Space Needle are two creations of the 1960's (top, left). A monorail (below) speeds away from the Seattle Center, with the Space Needle in the background. Both structures were built for the 1962 World's Fair that Seattle hosted.*

This page: *The glass facade of a modern office building near Seattle Center reflects nearby structures. The top of the Space Needle offers a revolving restaurant and bar as well as an outside observation deck. Spectacular views in all directions!*
Below: *A fountain at Seattle's Pacific Science Center, with the Space Needle in the background.*

But they did try. In the early 1960's, developers wanted to replace the old buildings with expensive retail space and high-rise housing (the views of Elliott Bay and the Olympics are magnificent.) Victor Steinbrueck, a local architect, lead a grass-roots organization called Friends of the Market that succeeded in saving the old place and preserving it as a historic district.

To savor the best of the market, rise early and be on hand by 7:30 or 8:00 in the morning (it's an easy walk from downtown hotels.) Fruit and vegetable vendors will be unloading trucks, building display mountains of tomatoes, cucumbers, carrots, lettuce, apples, oranges, radishes, onions, eggplant and just about every other kind of fresh produce you can imagine, all the while calling to each other and passersby in accents of Greek, Italian, Japanese, Spanish, and half a dozen other tongues. At the north end of the upper level, craftspeople will be laying out their day's display of handmade jewelry, weaving, carving, or glasswork.

Descending the stairs beneath the market (Pike Place Hillclimb), one finds the waterfront at Pier 61 or 62. To the right, working piers extend a half-mile or so to Pier 70, a refurbrished shedlike wharf that now contains informal restaurants, and crafts shops. The three ships that make the run to Victoria depart from Pier 69.

To explore the entire waterfront, catch one of the cream-and-white trolleys that clang past every few minutes. The trolleys were brought from Melbourne, Australia, and installed in 1982 as the inspired project of one man—City Councilman, "Streetcar" George Benson. A 60-cent ticket allows you to ride for two hours.

Heading south, you'll reach Pier 59, Waterfront Park (splendid views and picture-taking), the Omnidome and Seattle Aquarium. A plaque set in the concrete guardrail along the sidewalk marks the spot where the steamer *Portland* landed with that famous ton of gold in 1897.

Though the Seattle Aquarium displays a wide variety of tropical fish and indigenous species accompanied by excellent interpretive panels that explain everything from fish life cycles to water pollution, the *pièce de résistance* is a huge viewing dome beneath Elliott Bay. You stand inside the windowed dome and the fish view you. The sea otter and harbor seal exhibits always captivate, and there's plenty of action as salmon climb the fish ladder during summer and fall spawning runs.

Pier 53 is the home of Seattle's two fireboats, the *Duwamish* and the *Sealth.* They conduct their weekly practice in Elliott Bay, creating rainbows as their powerful nozzles jet fountains of water high in the air.

Pioneer Square is a triangular area featuring an ornate old iron pergola and totem pole surrounded by handsome stone Victorian-era business buildings. But when most Seattleites refer to Pioneer Square, they mean the entire historic district to the south. The 20-plus blocks in the historic district contain the city's best galleries, several fine bookstores, and dozens of specialty shops and excellent restaurants.

Fisherman's Terminal is where most of the hundreds of fishing vessels that home port in Seattle and fish as far north as the Bering Strait are moored. Early morning is a good time to see the fleet when fishermen are repairing nets, loading stores, and overhauling gear. Boats sometimes sell fish from the docks and the marine supply store here is an excellent place to pick up nautical books, charts, and fixtures. Across the ship canal is Ballard, Seattle's Scandinavian neighborhood strong on traditions of fishing and lumbering. When, early in the century, engineers cut the ship canal across Seattle's waist to provide deep-water access for ocean-going ships to the fresh water of Lake Washington, they had to install locks to compensate for the approximately 21-foot difference between tidal salt-water and the canal. The Hiram M. Chittenden Locks today provide a fascinating show that goes on nearly 24 hours a day.

An astonishing number of otherwise well-informed Americans, who have never been to the Pacific Northwest, are under the impression that Seattle is on the Pacific Ocean. It is not. The Pacific Coast is some 90 miles (as the seagull flies) west of Seattle. The land that lies in between—the Olympic Peninsula—is some of the wildest, most ruggedly beautiful country on the North American continent.

Top to bottom: *Pike Place Market is located in the heart of Seattle's downtown, and fresh fish and produce are available year-round. Salmon, crabs, and fresh flowers are just some of the goods residents and tourists can shop for from early morning until sunset. Waterfront Park, near ferry terminals and port traffic, provides a quiet place to view the Puget Sound or the city skyline.*

The waterfront. Shops, walkways, and bridges make up much of Pier 57, along with a large deck where public fishing is allowed. Bottom: The Virginia V takes passengers on sunset cruises around Puget Sound. Opposite: Its imaginative design and iridescent blue facade make the Washington Mutual Tower (left) a welcome addition to Seattle's skyline. Once the highest skyscraper west of the Mississippi, Smith Tower (right), built in 1914, still stands tall but is overshadowed by buildings twice its height. Below: The view many ferry commuters enjoy on their way into Seattle from nearby islands.

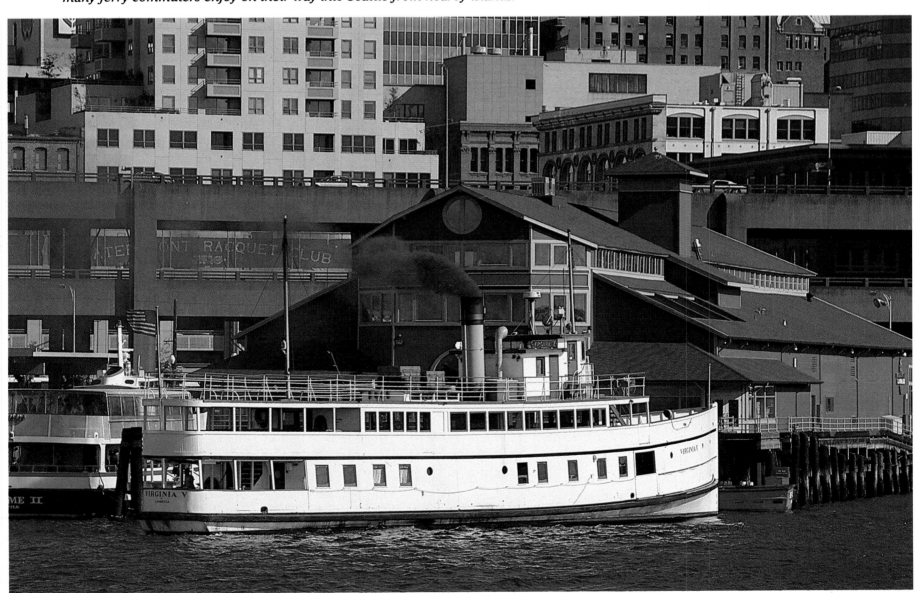

Sticking up like a giant thumb, the peninsula has a salubrious effect on Puget Sound country. It acts as a rain shelter, shielding the land to the east from much of the wind and moisture that sweep into the coast from the Gulf of Alaska. On the west side of the peninsula rainfall reaches averages of more than 100 inches annually. By contrast, Seattle receives a mere 35 inches and several places on the eastern side of the peninsula (in the "rain shadow") get only about 16 or 17 inches.

The other thing that characterizes the Olympic Peninsula is its geographical isolation. Olympic National Park occupies most of the peninsula and the only way to reach its mountainous interior is on foot; no roads penetrate beyond a few miles. U.S. 101 circles the peninsula with short spur roads leading to portions of the park and the beaches.

Still, its very remoteness makes it a fascinating destination and one of the few places left in this country where you can sample land that has not changed very much from the way it was when the first explorers discovered it.

❧ ❧ ❧

Tacoma, Seattle's neighbor city to the south, is a major deepwater port focusing on horseshoe-shaped Commencement Bay. Forest products processing and export facilities dominate the waterfront except for a short stretch with fashionable restaurants along Ruston Way.

Two primary sights in Tacoma are the Washington State Historical Society Museum and Point Defiance Park. Point Defiance Park is the first urban park in the state and (along with Portland's Washington Park and Vancouver's Stanley Park) one of the three finest in the Pacific Northwest.

The Seattle Art Museum, in Volunteer Park (top, left), houses an impressive collection of Asian art. The University of Washington campus (top, right) has a number of park-like walks, including the quad where cherry trees bloom in the spring. The Japanese Gardens (Below) in the University of Washington's Arboretum, is a place of quiet delights.

The south end of Seattle (top, left) makes up most of its working harbor, where giant containers move between ship and rail for both domestic and international trade. The Kingdome (top, right), Seattle's largest covered sports arena. In hilly Gasworks Park (below), off Lake Union, an old gasworks due for demolition has now become an "industrial sculpture."

Preceding page: *A container ship with a tugboat is a common sight in Puget Sound, where cargo is loaded and unloaded from nearby piers.* This page: *More of maritime Seattle—Fisherman's Terminal.*

Fort Nisqually, a restored Hudson's Bay fur trading post (c. 1833), contains the oldest building in the state as well as exhibits detailing the rugged life there in the nineteenth century. Camp Six recreates a typical logging camp and includes a steam locomotive that operates on summer weekends. Large portions of the 698-acre park have been preserved as a coastal forest with 200-foot-tall Douglas firs, groves of cedar, giant native rhododendrons that stand 10 feet tall, and lush forest glens carpeted with moss and ferns. Hiking trails, bicycle paths, and a five-mile drive take you through the best of the forest.

One of Washington's most curious sites lies just outside the park. From the bluff at Fort Nisqually you look down on Tacoma Narrows, a slender waterway spanned by a soaring suspension bridge—at 188 feet high and with a center span of 2,800 feet, it is one of the largest in the world. However, the curiosity is not the present bridge, but the previous one. On November 7, 1940, four months and seven days after it had opened, the original Tacoma Narrows Bridge collapsed, a victim of strong winds and structural harmonics that caused the locals to name it "Galloping Gertie." Needless to say, the engineers who built it were a bit embarrassed, but no more so than the insurance agent who had insured the bridge. Secure in the knowledge that nothing would ever happen to such a substantial structure, he had pocketed the insurance premiums!

Washington, in fact, seems to have a predilection for building "indestructible" bridges that then astonish the engineers by collapsing. Tacoma's "Galloping Gertie" was one of the first; Hood Canal Bridge was another. Both the present toll bridge and the original are (and were) floating pontoon bridges built over salt water—quite an engineering accomplishment when you consider the tidal fluctuation often exceeds 15 feet. The engineers who built the first one guaranteed that only a virtually impossible combination of wind, storm, and tide would have any effect on the bridge. On February 13, 1979, the impossible occurred and about half of it sank into Hood Canal. A brand-new bridge has been built to replace it. It, too, is "indestructible."

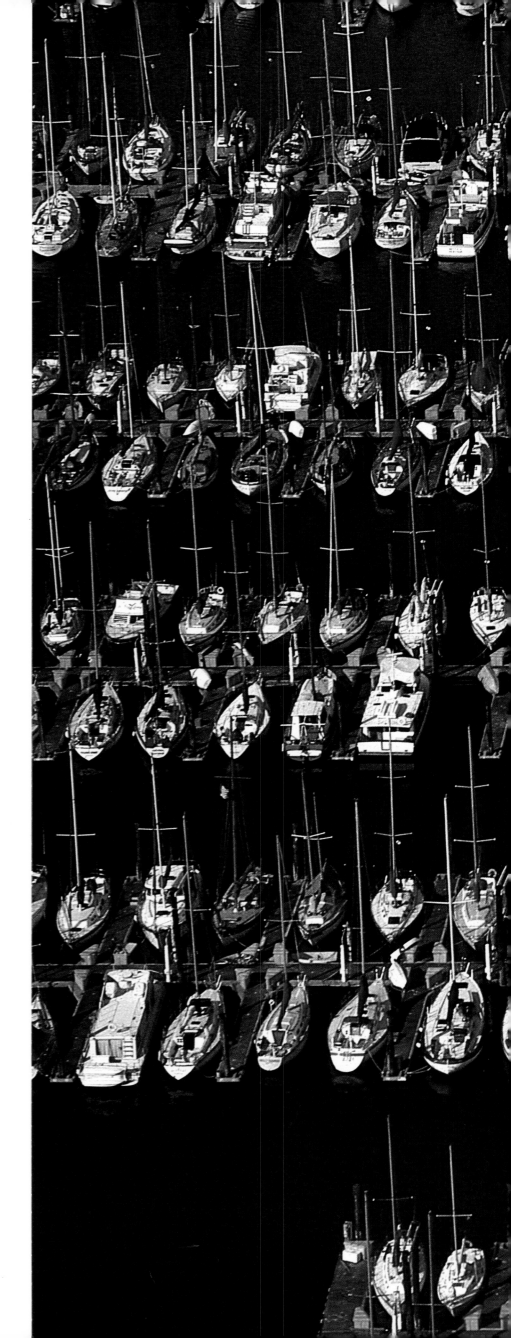

❧ ❧ ❧

Port Gamble is a lumber company town that seems frozen in time: the turn of the century. Puget Sound was once dotted with dozens of company towns (most of them named Port), where timber was milled and the lumber shipped aboard schooners. Port Gamble is the only one left in anywhere near its original condition. There are quiet streets lined with New England-style frame houses and a white steepled church, a replica of one in East Machias, Maine. The old general store stocks every imaginable kind of merchandise and has a large seashell collection upstairs.

Another port town, Port Townsend, is a living museum, with the best collection of Victorian architecture north of San Francisco. Once a strong rival of Seattle, this town perched at the entrance to Puget Sound boomed and faded in the 1890's.

Shilshole Bay Marina, Puget Sound.

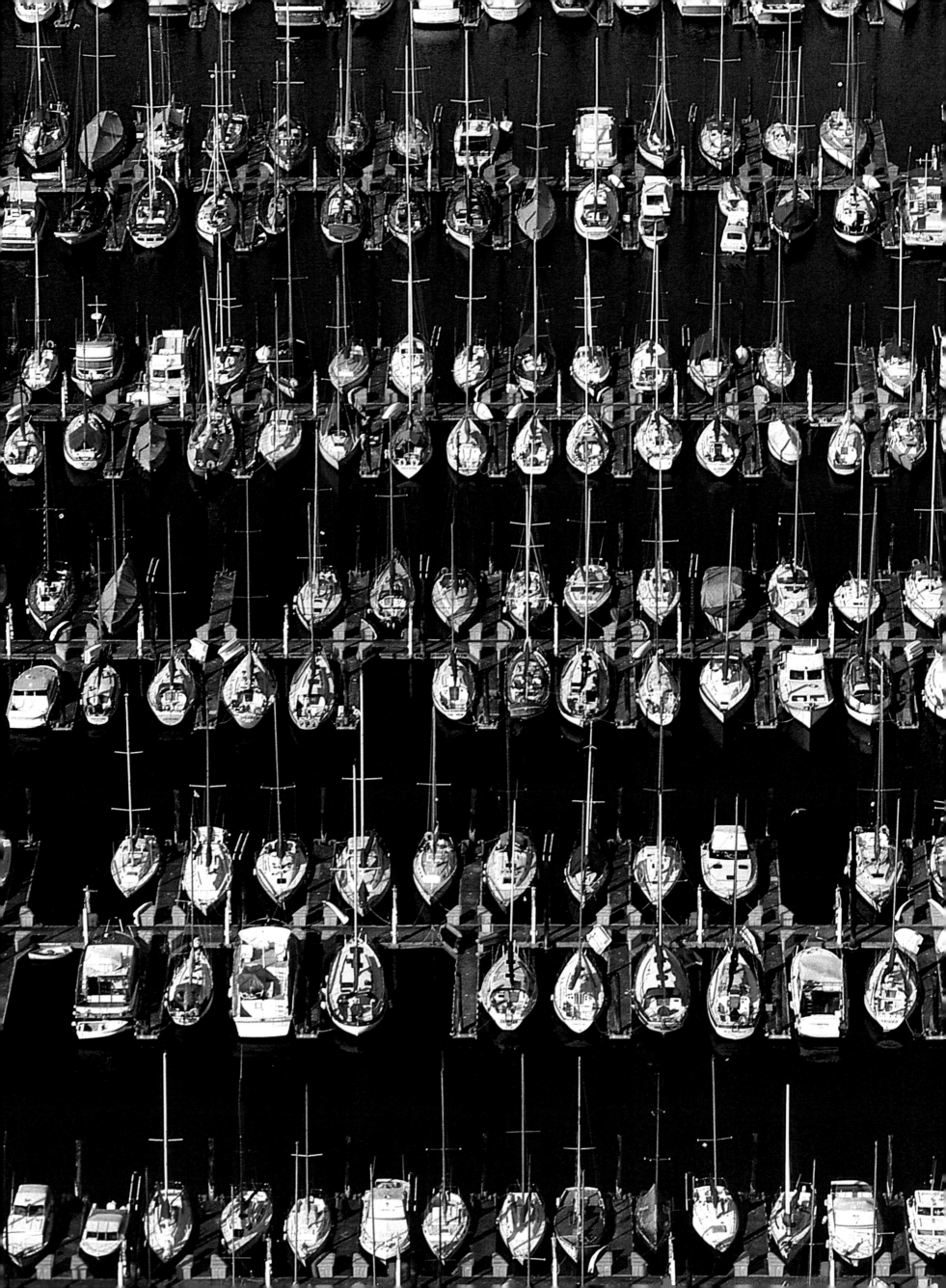

Downtown streets are lined with substantial sandstone and brick business buildings surmounted with turrets, ironwork, and plasterwork. Castle-like Jefferson County Courthouse surmounts a hill overlooking the harbor. In recent years the town has become a mecca for artists, craftsmen, and wooden boat builders. Many of the ornate old homes have been restored and some converted to bed-and-breakfast inns.

A mile west of town, Fort Worden, another in the chain of coastal defense forts that once guarded Puget Sound, is now a state park that preserves the old parade ground, officer's quarters, administration buildings, and barracks.

As U.S. 101 swings around the top of the Olympic peninsula, it passes through Sequim, a small town that is rapidly becoming a retirement center, chiefly because of its salubrious "banana belt" climate. Dungeness Spit, the longest sandspit in the U.S., juts six miles into the Strait of Juan de Fuca and harbors more than 250 species of waterfowl and shorebirds. A national wildlife refuge has marked trails and observation points.

❧ ❧ ❧

Most visitors see Olympic National Park for the first time from the lofty (5,757-foot) viewpoint of Hurricane Ridge. From the observation point at Heart O'Hills Highway, you look south into the heart of the 1,420-square-mile park, a spectacular jumble of jagged snow-clad peaks cut by steep timbered river valleys. On a clear day you'll be able to pick out the tallest peaks—Mount Olympus (7,965 feet), Mount Deception (7,788 feet), and Mount Anderson (7,332 feet). At Hoh Rain Forest, trails lead from the visitor center through a damp green cathedral that receives as much as 200 inches of rainfall a year.

Moss-covered trees add to the ethereal beauty of the Olympic Rain Forest. Vines, ferns, and moss cling to the trunks of giant trees like the mighty Oxalist Hemlock. Opposite: Lake Quinault, in Olympic National Park, offers swimming, fishing, and boating and has lake resorts scattered along its shores. Overleaf: Mount Olympus, the highest mountain in the range, with an alpine tarn.

Previous page: *During the summer months, the bare rock of Mount Olympus (top) can be seen rising from the lush rain forest. Made up of sandstone and slate, the Olympic Mountains have an icy core and a number of active glaciers flowing from their upper reaches (below).* This page: *In winter, thick clouds hover below its summit. Weather patterns often shift as storms come up against this formidable mountain range (top). The Blue Glacier on Mount Olympus reaches its dramatic end, while changing temperatures keep its mounds of snow and ice in motion (below).*

These pages: *The Olympic Peninsula's spectacular beaches, and the seastacks off Cape Flattery.*

Giant seastacks dot the shores of the Olympic Peninsula off *Rialto Beach.* Below: *An old shipwreck at low tide, a reminder of what rough weather does along the rocky shores of Cape Flattery.*

BRITISH COLUMBIA

The word "unique" is overused, but it certainly applies to Victoria. Victoria is one-of-a-kind, unlike anyplace else in this corner of the continent.

Unfortunately, for Victorians and for the rest of us, the city has suffered under the label, "A Little Bit of Olde England," until most people who love and respect Victoria are a bit nauseated by the term. The huckster who dreamed up the England-look-alike promotion should be condemned to an advertising hall for the infamous.

Except for a few touches like double-decker London excursion buses, lots of formal gardens, tea in the afternoon, and Sunday cricket matches, Victoria is not like England. It is conservative in dress and architecture, perhaps a bit stuffy when it comes to nightlife and entertainment, but absolutely comfortable, a bit like an old friend you haven't seen in years.

Float planes fly from both Seattle and Vancouver to land in Victoria's Inner Harbour, right in front of the Empress Hotel. Land-based planes arrive at Victoria International Airport, about 12 miles north of the city. You can travel on any of the ferries as a foot passenger; frequent intercity buses operate between Vancouver and Victoria via ferry. Most of the city's attractions are clustered in a relatively small area, easy for walking.

Sightseeing in Victoria begins and ends on the seawall fronting the Inner Harbour. Sightseeing buses and "tally-ho" horse-drawn sightseeing carriages depart from here.

Whether or not you stay there, you can't ignore the massive old Empress Hotel. Wander through its ornate lobby, heavy with oak and brass. Stop for curry in the Bengal Lounge or tea in the lobby (4:00 p.m.) In the northern end of the building, Miniature World depicts famous battles, Dickensian England, and other scenes with animated miniatures, including an extensive railway.

South, across Belleville Street, is the royal Provincial Museum. The intricate large-scale sculpture of Native Americans on a whaling expedition that stands in the foyer is a favorite. There are three floors of exhibits depicting British Columbian human and natural history. Especially good are the extensive collections of Native American artifacts, the forest and seashore life-like dioramas and the historical walk-through exhibits of a salmon cannery and nineteenth-century village.

In the same block is Thunderbird Park, with its colorful collection of totem poles. Native American carvers can be seen at work on new poles during the summer months. Helmcken House, behind the museum, was the home of a Hudson's Bay Company doctor and dates from 1852. It's furnished with many of the original pieces.

British Columbia's ornate old Parliament Buildings are set amid carefully-tended formal gardens and outlined at night with 3,300 light bulbs. The buildings resemble similar structures in Copenhagen's Tivoli Gardens; they were designed by a 25-year-old British architect, Francis Mawson Rattenbury, and illuminated for the first time on June 21, 1897, to celebrate Queen Victoria's Diamond Jubilee. The interior has many lovely stained-glass windows, including the famous Victoria Jubilee window, floor mosaics, murals, and woodcarvings.

Also, on the south side of the harbor along Belleville Street, you'll find the dock for steamships and catamarans from Seattle, the Royal London Wax Museum, and the Pacific Undersea Gardens, the latter with an observation room beneath the surface of the harbor. There's a constant procession of small boats, tugs, barges, and even seaplanes criss-crossing the Inner Harbour. Harbor tours depart from the city wharf in front of the Empress Hotel and take a little over an hour to cover seven miles past Fisherman's Wharf, Olde Town, and the Coast Guard station.

The Emily Carr Gallery features the works of British Columbia's most prominent artist as well as changing exhibits. Next door, Bastion Square commemorates the site where James Douglas established Fort Victoria in 1843. The Maritime Museum is there, housed in the former Provincial Law Courts building. The museum features ship models, two historic vessels, as well as uniforms and paintings of maritime scenes.

Down Wharf Street is Market Square, a block of nine restored nineteenth-century buildings that now house shops and restaurants. Across the street is the Esquimalt and Nanaimo Railway (VIA Rail) depot where you can catch the daily scenic train up island to Nanaimo and Courtenay. Just beyond is Victoria's diminutive Chinatown, a block of restaurants and stores along Fisgard Street delineated by the ornate Gate of Harmonious Interest.

Behind the Empress lies Crystal Garden, a lovely tropical conservatory with walks winding through tropical plantings, past a stream and waterfall. There's also an aviary populated with songbirds.

At 1401 Rockland Avenue Government House, the official residence of British Columbia's Lieutenant Governor, sits amid 35 acres of beautifully landscaped grounds open to the public. Nearby Craigdarroch Castle may be reminiscent of similar buildings seen in Scotland. Built of sandstone by a wealthy Scottish industrialist in the 1880's, the mansion contains fine works of art, stained- and leaded-glass windows and lavish furnishings.

Butchart is located 13 miles north of Victoria off B.C. 17. Compared favorably with England's Kew Gardens, Butchart annually attracts thousands of visitors who expose uncounted rolls of color film and, inspired by what they see, take home tons of seeds, plants and garden manuals to try to duplicate a little of its beauty at home. It doesn't matter in which season Butchart visited, plantings are changed regularly and the 35 acres of former rock quarry always seems to be in spectacular bloom.

Preceding page, counterclockwise from top: *Indian tribes of the Pacific Northwest erected totem poles, often in front of their dwellings. The animals or natural objects carved on the poles were considered ancestrally related to the group. Totem pole atop a hill overlooking Qualicum Beach, Vancouver Island.* This page: *On Vancouver Island, a logging bus on a dirt road, and the Douglas firs that make up much of the beautiful forest in Cathedral Grove.*

Buchart Gardens, near Victoria, has 35 acres of flowers from all over the world. Opposite, top: *Victoria (left), famous for its English flavor and love of flowers, has many Tudor-style houses. The elegant Empress Hotel (right) near the inner harbor is popular with tourists.* Below: *Fable Cottage Estate is a fantasy world of Cotswold-style houses and animated scenes that children of all ages love.*

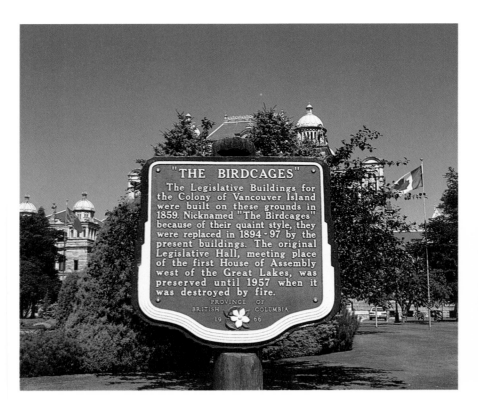

The late Victorian-era legislative buildings on Vancouver Island are set amid beautiful gardens. At the main entrance, a statue of Queen Victoria. Below: *Visitors to Victoria's Parliament building can take a guided tour up to the dome in the rotunda.* Opposite and overleaf: *Victoria's Parliament illuminated and the inner harbor, with its lighted docks, in the foreground.*

Preceding pages: *Often referred to as Canada's "Gem of the Pacific," Vancouver, B.C. enjoys an exquisite natural setting.* This page, top: *Fascinating stone sculpture can be found near the harbor and the city's main shopping area is close by.* Below: *Vancouver's English Bay.* Opposite: *Grouse Mountain, only 20 minutes away by car from Vancouver's high-rises, offers excellent skiing facilities.*

Also north and west of downtown are the extensive formal gardens of the Royal Roads Military College and Anne Hathaway's Cottage, a replica of Shakespeare's birthplace on the grounds of the Olde England Inn. Fable Cottage is one of those curiosities, a home and gardens constructed to resemble the setting of a fairy tale, complete with animated gnomes and a one-ton revolving flower basket.

On the southern perimeter of Victoria, Dallas Road and Beach Drive provide sweeping views of the Strait of Juan de Fuca, with the Olympic Mountains rising in the distance. The residential gardens in these neighborhoods are among the best in British Columbia and are especially lovely in April, May, and June when daffodils, tulips, rhododendrons, and azaleas are blooming.

Vancouver Island stretches for another 275 miles northward from Victoria, much of it semiwilderness, dominated by mountains and carpeted with thick evergreen forests.

It's 70 miles via Trans-Canada #1 to Nanaimo. The highway winds through the countryside, then climbs over Malahat Summit for sweeping views across the Saanich Peninsula to Mount Baker in Washington State.

The British Columbia Forest Museum in Duncan features logging demonstrations, historic logging equipment, and a steam locomotive-powered logging railroad.

Chemainus has become locally famous in recent years for the huge murals depicting its history painted on the walls of the town's buildings. Yellow footsteps painted on the sidewalk lead to the murals and you can pick up a guide booklet that describes the works and their artists. Ladysmith, a coal mining

Preceding page: *A statue of Captain George Vancouver (top), who was the first to circumnavigate Vancouver Island; he also explored and named Puget Sound. English Bay (bottom) at twilight.* This page: *Vancouver's skyline, a dazzling blend of glass-and-steel skyscrapers and grand old Victorian buildings.*

Preceding page: *Vancouver's Coal Harbor features a number of marinas and yacht clubs.* This page: *The* Island Princess *passes beneath Lions Gate Bridge, which connects Stanley Park and West Vancouver.*

and forest products town founded during the Boer War and named for the South African city, has several photogenic old buildings, locomotives, logging equipment, and a logging museum at Crown Forest Arboretum.

Nanaimo has preserved one of the bastions from its history as a Hudson's Bay Company fur trading post. The Centennial Museum features Native American, pioneer, and coal mining displays. The town hosts a major Shakespearean festival for 10 weeks in July and August each year.

Huge (nearly 500,000 acres) Stathcona Provincial Park occupies the central part of Vancouver Island west of Campbell River. The park is largely heavily forested wilderness, but contains several large lakes ideal for canoeing. There are campgrounds and a lodge in the park.

❧ ❧ ❧

For magnificent settings, it's tough to match Vancouver. When the world's most beautiful cities are listed—San Francisco, Sydney, Hong Kong, Paris—Vancouver, with its salt water nearly ringing the city and towering mountains forming a rugged backdrop, is often ranked right up there among the favorites. If you approach by ferry from Vancouver Island or the Sunshine Coast to Horseshoe Bay, you'll see great rocky mountains that nearly enclose the harbor, rising sheer from the water in battlements that tower thousands of feet over the city.

The similarities to San Francisco don't end with the abundance of water and the splendid scenery. More than any other Western city except San Francisco, Vancouver is a real cultural melting pot. Settled first by Scots, Irish, and English, later came citizens of the British Empire—Indians, Pakistanis, Hong Kong Chinese, New Zealanders, Australians, South Africans and other former colonials. More recently have come eastern Europeans, mainland Chinese, Japanese, southeast Asians, Pacific Islanders, and Latin Americans.

Downtown Vancouver lies on a peninsula with English Bay to the west, First Narrows to the north, and Burrard Inlet to the east. One thousand-acre Stanley Park occupies the tip of the peninsula; False Creek, along which Expo 86 was held, flanks the southern edge of downtown. Avenues in Vancouver run east and west, streets run north and south.

Alex Fraser Bridge, Port Mann Bridge, and Lions Gate Bridge. Each with a unique look, the bridges in and around the city connect over 796 square miles of Metropolitan Vancouver. Opposite: Modern high-rises dominate the skyline.

Located in Vancouver's downtown area at the north end of the Cambie Street Bridge, Canada Place Pavilion hosts a number of special events and sport spectaculars.

The old Vancouver Expo 86 "golf ball" has been converted into a center for hands-on science exhibits and hourly science shows. Near the waterfront, a statue of an athlete.

Preceding page: *Robson Square has something for everyone: art exhibits, concerts, ice skating, and—in summer—street entertainment.* This page: *Vancouver's Art Gallery (top) is now housed in the Old Court House. Behind it, the imposing Hotel Vancouver.* Right: *On Burrard Street, the glass exterior of a new office building reflects other nearby buildings.*

127

Gastown, the old, original heart of the city, grew south from the shore of Burrard Inlet beginning in 1867. It's named after a colorful saloon proprietor of the early days, "Gassy" Jack Deighton. Most of the handsome brick and stone buildings you see today postdate the fire of 1886, which all but destroyed the city. Serious restoration of the old buildings began in 1971, and subsequently the area became one of the most popular in the city with shops, restaurants, those very English streets called mews, and a lively nightlife.

Cheek-by-jowl with Gastown is Chinatown, said to be North America's second-largest urban Chinese settlement (after San Francisco), centered on Pender and Keefer Streets. The district is so ethnically Chinese that the McDonald's on Main Street displays its readerboard menu in Chinese. It's a great place for leisurely poking about. The Sam Kee Building at Carrall and Pender claims to be the narrowest office building in the world, at six feet wide. Stop to view Chinese art at the Chinese Cultural Centre and the lovely Sun Yat Sen Garden behind it.

In two short years, Canada Place has become the same kind of visual symbol of Vancouver that the Sydney Opera House has for that city. Architecturally stunning, it resembles a huge ocean liner surmounted by massive stylized sails. Built to house the federal government's exhibit at Expo 86, it is now the city's trade and convention center and cruise ship terminal; it also houses the Pan Pacific Hotel.

There are several buildings downtown from which you can get a bird's-eye view of Vancouver; the glass elevators at the Hyatt Regency Hotel or the Sears Store at Harbour Centre. The Harbour Centre skywalk and revolving restaurant have fine views, as do the revolving restaurants atop the Sheraton Landmark Hotel and New World Harbourside Hotel.

Robson Street has changed over the years. Once called Robsonstrasse, a street of small shops with a European flavor, it has gained in social status (as well as in price) with the addition of more trendy upscale restaurants and retailers (Polo Ralph Lauren, Alfred Sung, Ferragamo, French and Italian imports). The public market in the 1600 block is a bright colorful place, filled with fresh fruit and vegetable stands, cheese shops, a pie shop, fishmongers, a dessert store, and dozens of other purveyors of goodies.

At the southern edge of downtown, across False Creek, Granville Island has been rehabilitated from a former industrial area to a busy collection of galleries, arts and crafts shops, live theaters, restaurants, and a hotel. Centerpiece of the island is the Public Market, with its fruit and vegetable stands, flower shops, and food stalls. The island is accessible by car or by pedestrian passenger ferries, one departing from Vanier Park in Kitsilano, the other from a dock beneath the Granville Bridge.

One of Vancouver's many impressive structures is the City Hall with its stone-faced clock. Like many cities, Vancouver has a mix of architectural styles and little space left to build, so new uses are often found for old buildings. Flower beds brighten the entrance to the Cultural Center. Opposite: Gastown, Vancouver's historic corner of town, is a popular tourist attraction. Old red brick buildings house restaurants and shops, including the Inuit Gallery which sells Eskimo art.

Stanley Park combines beaches, woodlands, greensward, jogging and biking trails, a zoo, an aquarium, and splendid views of the city skyline in one big thousand-acre preserve, adjacent to downtown. There's a loop road through the park as well as dozens of miles of footpaths. Cricket matches, lawn bowling tournaments, and the evening gun fired each sun-down, are reminders that Vancouver is not in the United States. Have a morning breakfast snack or afternoon tea on Saturday at the Prospect Point Café overlooking First Narrows, and watch one of the great cruise ships sail beneath Lion's Gate Bridge on its way to or from Alaska.

Queen Elizabeth Park's 121 acres is partially sited in a former rock quarry atop Little Mountain, which isn't a mountain at all, but its lofty 400-foot elevation does allow you sweeping views of the city. Highlight of this park is Bloedel Conservatory. Beneath its triodetic dome grow hundreds of varieties of exotic plants in leafy profusion, in mini-climates ranging from tropical to desert. Free-flying birds flit past your ears as you wander through the conservatory. Van Dusen Botanical Gardens are intensively landscaped with 39 different sections, including formal, fragrance, and children's gardens. Seasonal blooms are showcased here.

Preceding page: *A statue of an early settler presides over a corner in Gastown.* **Bottom:** *One of the area's notable land-marks is a steam clock which lets out a hoot and a rush of steam as it tells the time.* This page: *Residents of Vancouver's Chinatown, the second largest in North America, celebrate the Lunar New Year. Chinatown offers visitors and residents some of the best restaurants anywhere, and its supermarkets, vegetable stalls, and bakeries stock the staples of many Asian cuisines.*

Preceding page: *The fountain in front of Vancouver's MacMillan Planetarium.* This page, top: *Dramatic fountains greet visitors to Vancouver's Bloedel Floral Conservatory, located on the highest point in the city, and a superb place to view all the sights.* Below: *The Vancouver Public Aquarium in Stanley Park has regularly scheduled whale shows and underwater viewing areas where visitors can watch these beautiful creatures up close.*

Totem poles such as these in Stanley Park were carved recently.
Nineteenth-century totem poles are too rare to be left outdoors
and consequently can be seen only in museums.

Vancouver is a fine town for museum exploring, with more than a dozen from which to choose. The Maritime Museum, Vancouver Museum, and H.R. MacMillan Planetarium are all situated in Vanier Park, overlooking English Bay. The Maritime Museum houses the *St. Roch,* the schooner on which a crew of Canadian Mounties sailed through the icebound Northwest Passage — in both directions — for the first time. As visitors walk the decks and poke about the cabins of the old ship, a tour guide explains the voyage and various ship's spaces. One marvels at the fortitude of the men who survived in such cramped quarters under miserable conditions for so long.

The Vancouver Museum concentrates on the city's history and includes extensive displays on Native American culture, fur trading days, and nineteenth-century development. MacMillan Planetarium features shows on space exploration and astronomy, as well as laser shows.

The University of British Columbia Museum of Anthropology is a fine museum devoted to the North Coastal Indians. Though totem poles are frequently encountered in Washington, British Columbia, and Alaska, many of them have been carved fairly recently. Authentic, historic totem poles from the nineteenth-century are rare and this museum probably has the best collection in existence. There are also extensive exhibits of Native American art, basketry, carvings, and artifacts. There are also cultural collections from Africa, the Pacific and the Americas.

This page: *Vancouver incorporates interesting architecture (above) with spectacular views of the surrounding waters (below).*

This page and opposite: *The challenging slopes of Whistler Mountain offer some of the best skiing in North America. In warmer weather, after the skiing season, its rugged terrain appeals to campers and hikers.*

These pages: *British Columbia's Garibaldi Provincial Park, 480,000 acres of awesome beauty, includes a snow-capped Atwell Peak.*

Preceding page: *Helmcken Falls in British Columbia's Wells Gray Provincial Park, known for its good fishing and excellent wilderness camping.* This page: *Fort Steele; its buildings, which date from 1873, and a walk down its main street remind us of simpler times.* Below: *A lookout station at historic Fort Steele, British Columbia.* Opposite: *An old community church also at Fort Steele.*

This page: *Kootenay National Park's Marble Canyon (left). Mixed conifer and larch forests fill the valley running north and south in the Kootenay National Park region (below). Opposite: The Kootenay River flows through a snowy valley.*

The Sunshine Coast, so named because it lies in the "rain shadow" of Vancouver Island and thus gets more sunshine, is a stretch of seaside resorts that clings to a narrow shelf of beach and land between the towering Coast Range and the waters of Malaspina Strait and the Strait of Georgia. Part of the Coast is the Sechelt Peninsula, where the road north winds its way through dense coastal forest—mostly cedars with a scattering of Douglas fir, spruce, and hemlock. Inspired by the beautiful scenery and lured by the quiet lifestyle, many artists and craftsmen have come here to live and work.

The coast is also tops among salmon anglers. Fishing takes place nearly year-round with winter and spring salmon running from October to April, followed by bluebacks and coho. The record salmon caught weighed 64 pounds and was hooked near Pender Harbour.

The Trans-Canada is a mighty highway, stretching across the continent from Pacific to Atlantic. It is Canada's premier highway and because this country has just one transcontinental highway, it assumes a great deal more importance than do the interstates of the U.S. It and two railways are the links that tie Canada together.

Its British Columbia section is the most spectacular of its several thousand-mile path. From Vancouver to the Alberta border atop Kicking Horse Pass is about 477 miles. (Mile zero on the Trans-Can is actually at the corner of Douglas Street and Dallas Road in Victoria.) Along the way it traverses some of the most rugged and beautiful country there is.

North of Hope, the highway threads its way through the sheer-walled Fraser River Canyon. Canada's two transcontinental railroads—the Canadian National and the Canadian Pacific—were here first. The tracks cling to the canyon walls, usually below the highway, and trade sides of the canyon as they plunge through tunnels and criss-cross it on spindly trestles.

Kamloops was a major supply point, first for the fur traders who came here in 1811, then for the thousands who trekked north to join the Cariboo Gold Rush in the 1860's.

Revelstoke, an important division point on Canada's first transcontinental railroad, the Canadian Pacific, is also headquarters for many types of backcountry vacations.

For the avid skier, the ultimate experience is helicopter skiing. Large helicopters lift as many as 12 skiers at a time to remote, isolated lodges in the Bugaboo, Monashee, and Selkirk mountains. The lodges are comfortable and include meals. Helicopters then take skiers to the tops of nearby mountains, where waist-deep powder snow lies unbroken until skis slide through it. Skiers descend under supervision and, once they reach the bottom, are helicoptered to the top of another virgin peak for another descent. In the summer, these same helicopter companies transport hikers.

Just east of Revelstoke, Mount Revelstoke National Park sprawls over a large area of alpine landscape, from meadows resplendent in wildflowers in July and August to jagged peaks encased in glaciers that never completely melt.

A wildflower meadow in Mount Revelstoke National Park in the Canadian Rockies.

A snowed-in Emerald Lake in Yoho National Park. The area is well named: Yoho is an Indian word for "how beautiful." Dogsledding is the best way to get around during the heavy snows. Opposite: Emerald Lake Lodge in summer, with Mount Burgess in the distance. Mount Michael (below) provides a massive backdrop for canoers on the lake.

Dominated by 11,122-foot Mount Dawson, Glacier National Park occupies more than 520 square miles of spectacular mountain scenery. As its name implies, the park has more than 400 glaciers. It's worth a stop off the highway to drive to its scenic viewpoints, glimpse its wildlife and attend one of the interpretive programs that describe these subranges of the Rockies. Perhaps the most important feature of Glacier is Rogers Pass, where Trans-Canada 1 crests at 4,353 feet. There's a twin-arched monument at the summit, and a visitor center. To the south, east and west stretch rank upon rank of lofty forested mountains and deep valleys. This country is so rugged that this last link in the Trans-Canada highway was not completed until the early 1960's.

Golden is a mountain town. For campers, it is a good place to stop for supplies, and a nice quiet spot for a night or two while exploring the surrounding country. East of Golden, the highway begins its long climb to the little railroad town of Field (where they put on helper engines for the steep grade) and Kicking Horse Pass. On its ascent of the 5,390-foot pass, the railroad transits two spiral tunnels, looping over itself twice to climb several hundred feet with limited forward progress. This has been acclaimed as one of the engineering wonders of the world; viewpoints and interpretive signs are located above the tunnels.

Everyone knows about the Canadian Rockies. Hollywood motion pictures, travel agents and tour companies extol their virtues. In Yoho National Park is the Takakkaw Falls (one of the highest in North America) plunging 1,259 feet in a crashing display of mist and rainbows; also seen are the rushing Kicking Horse River, mirror-like Emerald Lake, and dozens of monumental peaks. Kootenay is the gentler of the two parks, cut by a long, forested valley and meadows carpeted in tall grass. Here moose, elk, deer, bear and other wildlife are likely to be seen. Near its southern entrance, Radium Hot Springs has thermal baths and overnight accommodations catering to visitors.

❧ ❧ ❧

In the summers of centuries past, the Native Canadians of British Columbia came to the Okanagan Valley to fish, to trade and to feast. Flanked by rank upon rank of mountains—the Canadian Rockies to the east, the Coast Range to the west— forests open into a lovely 175-mile long valley of sparkling lakes, lots of sunshine and hills carpeted with vineyards, orchards and golf courses.

O'Keefe Historic Ranch, founded in 1897 and now a museum, is typical of the vast cattle spreads that once occupied this part of the province. But the Okanangan derives its real wealth from its orchards and vineyards. Rich soil and a climate similar to Germany's Rhine River Valley make this Canada's second-largest wine-producing region, after the Niagara Frontier. More than 50 vineyards, primarily in the southern half of the valley, furnish grapes (mostly white) to several wineries.

Preceding page: *View of the top of Takakkaw Falls in Yoho National Park.* This page: *Rainbows and waterfalls grace the mountain peaks in the Yoho National Park region.* Overleaf: *Magic Lake reflects Mount Assiniboine, part of the Canadian Rockies.*

Mount Assiniboine and environs. Layers of sediment create a colorful pattern along the Rocky Mountains, with the sandy base of this region resembling an eerie moonscape. Opposite: British Columbia's Mount Assiniboine is an Alps look-alike with its handsome snow-covered cone. Overleaf: Mount Assiniboine Provincial Park. Wedgewood Peak stands near Lake Megog, Sunburst and Cerulean lakes, with Mount Assiniboine in the distance.

Previous pages, top: *Asulkan Glacier makes up only a small part of Glacier National Park's spectacular array of ice fields.* Previous pages, bottom: *Intersecting arches call attention to a plaque that gives information for those crossing Rogers Pass. A scenic turnoff on the Trans-Canada Highway, near Rogers Pass, which is considered by many to offer the best view of Canada's Glacier National Park.* Preceding page: *The summit of Rogers Pass.* This page and opposite: *Mount Robson (top) towers above Berg Lake Trail (below). Mount Robson Provincial Park with Berg Lake and Berg Glacier, now part of the park.*

This page and opposite: *A guide climbs toward a surface that looks promising for skiing. Helicopter skiiers descend a slope in the Canadian Rockies.*

The Fraser River, known now for its good fishing and scenic banks, once attracted more than 30,000 gold-seekers to Canada. Right: Logging is one of British Columbia's most important industries. Here, logs are moved by water near the town of Savona. Opposite: Trains are protected from rock slides along Fraser Canyon by shoots built over the tracks. Overleaf: Mist and fog hang over British Columbia's Pacific coast.

British Columbia's Queen Charlotte Islands sit north of Vancouver Island. Damp and lush, this area rivals Norway's fjords in its beauty. Its rocky shores are a favorite gathering place for sea lions. Opposite: Western cedars reflected in a freshwater lake.

This page: *Totem Bight State Park House in Ketchikan, Alaska, offers a rich array of carved totems.*

ALASKA

The Alaskan coast is beautiful, but without any highways connecting most of the cities and towns in Southeast Alaska, the region (also known as the Panhandle) is best explored by cruise ship or by the ferries of the Alaska Marine Highway.

Juneau, Alaska's capital, is one of the most attractive cities in the state. The city itself is clustered along Gastineau Channel, a narrow canal-like waterway. The steep mountains just behind give rise to waterfalls that plunge down the cliff faces. Narrow streets that are a bit a-kilter (the city is less than 1/2-mile wide) give a haphazard look to downtown.

The capitol has to be the most nondescript state capitol of the 50. It looks like any other office building. The Alaska State Museum houses an extensive collection of native art, including baskets and carvings and the eagle tree, an eagle nesting tree that was moved intact into the museum and is the center of a nature display.

House of Wickersham, recently opened to the public, is the former residence of one of Alaska's early judges. He introduced the legislation that created Denali National Park, the Alaska Railroad, and the University of Alaska. Some items of his Alaskana collection are displayed in the home.

Diminutive St. Nicholas Russian Orthodox Church at 326 Fifth Street contains icons dating from the eighteenth century.

Mendenhall Glacier, 13 miles out of town, is a massive river of ice, 12 miles long and 1½ miles wide, and is especially awesome to walk atop.

❧ ❧ ❧

A town devoted to the fishing industry, Ketchikan is strung along the shore of Revillagigedo Island and is the first port of call in Alaska for most cruise ships plying the Inside Passage. Backdropped by steep mountains, the downtown area is essentially one long waterfront, about four blocks wide and four miles long.

The historic waterfront includes ship chandler's shops, fishing fleet facilities, art shops, and cafés. The city is noted for its fine totem poles, especially at the Totem Heritage Center across from the city park. Its 33 poles make up the largest collection of original totems in Alaska.

Creek Street is the city's former red-light district where brothels ran full blast as late as 1954. Some of the nearly 20 houses flanking Ketchikan Creek have been restored; several house art galleries and boutiques. Dolly's House is now a museum.

At the Tongass Historical Museum on Dock Street, displays are devoted to local Native American and pioneer history. On the Tongass Highway, just outside of town, is found Saxman Totem Park, with 22 totems, and Totem Bight community house and totem park, with a model of a Tlingit community house and another 13 totems.

Some cruise ships call at Misty Fjords National Monument, a 3,579-square-mile chunk of dramatic coastal scenery with abundant viewable wildlife, such as bears and bald eagles. Sightseeing boats and float planes depart from the Ketchikan waterfront for the 30 miles to the monument.

❧ ❧ ❧

Wrangell is another small city on an island (population 2,376) where the strong Native American heritage is evident the moment you step ashore. Totem poles, Native American designs, and public art relating to the Stikine and Tlingit Indians are displayed just about everywhere.

Chief Shakes Island and Community House has several excellent totems, a tribal house, and cultural displays of tools, blankets, and other items. Wrangell Museum, near the ferry terminal, exhibits prehistoric petroglyphs, pictographs, early photographs, Native American tools, and pioneer artifacts.

❧ ❧ ❧

A colorful logging and fishing settlement, Petersburg was largely settled by Scandinavians and is known locally as "little Norway" for its brightly colored wooden residences decorated with hand-painted designs.

The freshly caught seafood—shrimp, salmon, crab, halibut—on the menus of Petersburg restaurants is among the best in Alaska. Spawning salmon put on a show in August and September when they return to the creeks and rapids around town. Charter boats visit the Le Conte Glacier, 25 miles east, where the drama of a tidewater glacier "calving" can be seen at fairly regular intervals.

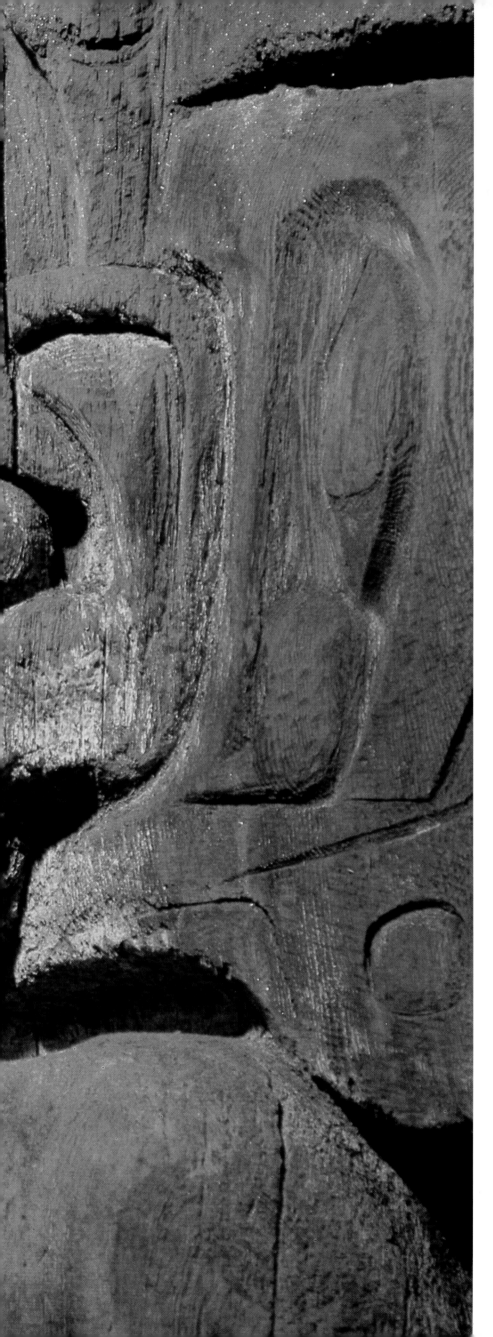

Many old Alaska hands have a soft spot in their hearts for Sitka. It was here that the Russians established the capital of their fur trading empire, New Archangel, in the first decade of the nineteenth century. Their leader, Alexander Baranof, was a colorful character whose name is encountered all over Alaska. When the Russians ceded Alaska to the United States in 1867, they did it in Sitka. Much evidence of the Russian occupation remains and Sitka rivals Skagway for the best historical sightseeing in Alaska.

The New Archangel dancers, dressed in Russian costumes, greet most cruise ships by performing authentic Russian dances.

Baranof Castle Hill Historic Site is where the ceremony transferring Alaska to the United States took place. Down the hill along the harbor is a Russian blockhouse, a replica of the original which settlers defended from the Tlingit Indians. It's worthwhile strolling through the old Russian cemetery to examine the gravestones, including one for Princess Maksoutoff.

Walking southeast along the harbor, you come to a gem of a Russian Orthodox church, St. Michael's Cathedral. The original burned in 1964, but this replica is authentic in detail and contains some exquisite antique icons, enameled porcelain, and other Russian church art. The Russian Bishop's House, a few blocks to the east, was built in 1842 and is one of the oldest buildings in Alaska.

The Isabel Miller Museum, located in the Centennial Building, has exhibits detailing the history of Sitka, including a large model of the city as it was in 1867. The Sheldon Jackson Museum, on the campus of Sheldon Jackson College, exhibits an outstanding collection of Inuit and Native American arts and crafts, most of it assembled by missionary Jackson.

At the southeastern end of town, Sitka National Historical Park preserves the 107-acre site of a 1904 battle between the Russians and their loyal native followers, and the Tlingit Indians. The park has 26 totem poles and its visitor center has historical exhibits.

❧ ❧ ❧

In the winter of 1897-1898, thousands of would-be prospectors—spurred by the discovery of gold in Canada's Klondike—jammed every ship heading north and crowded into the town of Skagway. A North West Mounted Police report of 1897 described the ramshackle town as "little more than hell on earth." The lusty town was one big collection of saloons, gambling halls, brothels and miner's outfitters. Many a tenderfoot never got beyond Skagway, fleeced of his savings by confidence men or gamblers or shot dead in one of the hundreds of saloon brawls.

Wood is abundant in the northwest, making it a natural material for Native Americans to use for their art and in their religious rites.

The old saloons and false-fronted stores are now part of Klondike Gold Rush National Historical Park (the southern section of which is in Seattle.) The notorious "Soapy" Smith may have died of gunshot wounds in 1898, but his spirit comes alive each summer evening in Skagway with the nightly performance of "Skagway in the Days of '98" at the Eagles Hall. You can visit his grave in Gold Rush Cemetery, learn more about Gold Rush history at the Trail of '98 Museum, and tour the town in horse- or dog-drawn vehicles.

Klondikers had to struggle up and over White or Chilcoot passes, often hauling the required 1,150 pounds of food and gear up the slopes one backbreaking load at a time. Once over the passes, these would-be prospectors still had more than 500 miles of treacherous river rapids and howling wilderness to go before they reached Dawson.

In Glacier Bay, ships pull within a mile of one of the most awesome sights in the north—the towering faces of tidewater glaciers. As passengers watch, the face crumbles and massive chunks of blue ice "calve" into the bay. Moments later a thunderous roar reaches the ears of passengers and a great swell moves slowly across the bay, leaving dozens of icebergs in its wake.

The national park contains 16 of these glaciers. Unless you are aboard a cruise ship, you can only reach it by boat or plane from Juneau, approximately 100 miles away.

❦ ❦ ❦ ❦ ❦

*T*he Pacific Northwest has some of the most spectacular scenery you'll ever encounter. Stand on the moss floor of the Hoh Rain Forest, moss-draped spruce towering overhead, and you'll swear the light filtering through the trees and ferns is actually green. Perch safely on the cliffs at Cape Kiwanda and the pounding surf will literally shake the earth beneath your feet. Relax in a deck chair as your cruise ship glides over the blue-black waters of the Inside Passage, and it will seem as if the forest-clad mountains rise directly from the sea.

Nowhere in North America is there so much incredible scenery accessible to the average traveler.

Centennial Hall serves as Juneau's convention center and offers multimedia presentations on the Tongass National Forest and Glacier Bay National Park and Preserve. This old log cabin is now a visitor's center in downtown Juneau, Alaska's capital and third-largest city. Although on the mainland, the city can't be reached directly by road—all car traffic in and out of town uses the Alaska Marine Highway ferry system. Opposite, top: In the late 1800's, Skagway was on the main route for Yukon gold prospectors. Klondike Gold Rush National Historical Park offers reminders of those days. Bottom: The city's Gold Rush Cemetery. Overleaf: Rainbow Glacier, near Haines, Alaska.

A salmon trawler off St. Lazaria Island in Sitka Sound. Below: *Mount Veristova.* Opposite: *Herring boats tie up in Sitka's harbor for the night.*

Preceding page: *Alaska's Russian heritage is apparent in Sitka, with St. Michael's Cathedral.* This page: *From cruise ships, Alaska's Inside Passage offers spectacular sights, including brilliant sunsets and occasional whale spottings.*

Aerial view of Southeast Alaska's glaciers.

The Statendam *passes Columbia Glacier, which is higher than a 20-story building and sheds millions of tons of ice every day. Opposite: Margerie Glacier in Glacier Bay is one of many ice-and-rock formations that abound in the inlets northwest of Juneau.*

This page: *The waterways through Glacier Bay National Park and Preserve provide access to more than 16 tidewater glaciers (top). When icebergs the size of 10-story buildings shift (bottom), tons of water and spray are sent skyward.* Opposite: *Glacier Bay was once a wall of ice, but with much of the ice melted over time, nearly 50 miles of fjords and islands are visible today.* Following pages: *Glacier Bay National Monument. Black rocks and creamy white hills make for a dramatic landscape at this rugged spot.*

Index of Photography

TIB indicates The Image Bank

Page Number	Photographer
Title page	Ric Ergenbright
2-3	Rick Schafer/Ray Atkeson Photography
6 (4)	Ray Atkeson Photography
7	Ed Cooper
8-9	Ray Atkeson Photography
10 top	Tom Mareschal/TIB
10 bottom	Ed Cooper
11	Ed Cooper
12 top left	Larry Geddis
12 top right	Hans Wendler/TIB
12 bottom	Ray Atkeson Photography
13 (2)	Ric Ergenbright
14	Ed Cooper
15 top	Larry Geddis
15 center	Ric Ergenbright
15 bottom	Ray Atkeson Photography
16 top	Tim Fitzharris
16 bottom	Ray Atkeson Photography
17 top	Larry Geddis
17 bottom	Vince Parrella/Stockphotos, Inc.
18	Ray Atkeson Photography
19	Larry Geddis
20-21	Ed Cooper
22 top	Ed Cooper
22 bottom	Larry Geddis
23 top	Rick Schafer/Ray Atkeson Photography
23 bottom	Ray Atkeson Photography
24-25	Russ Davies/Stockphotos, Inc.
26 top	Harald Sund/TIB
26 bottom	Ray Atkeson Photography
27	Ed Cooper
28 top	Larry Geddis
28 bottom	Ray Atkeson Photography
29	Rick Schafer/Ray Atkeson Photography
30-31	Ric Ergenbright
32	Larry Geddis
33 (2)	Ric Ergenbright
34-35	Ed Cooper
36	Larry Geddis
37	Larry Geddis
38-39	Ed Cooper
40 (2)	Larry Geddis
41	Ed Cooper
42 top	Tom & Pat Leeson
42 bottom	Ed Cooper
43	Rick Schafer/Ray Atkeson Photography
44 top	Larry Geddis
44 bottom	Andy Caulfield/TIB
45	Marc Solomon/TIB
46 top left	Larry Geddis
46 top right	Ray Atkeson Photography
46 bottom	Ray Atkeson Photography
47 top	Larry Geddis
47 center	Larry Geddis
47 bottom	David W. Hamilton/TIB
48 (2)	Larry Geddis
49 (2)	Rick Schafer/Ray Atkeson Photography
50 top	Ed Cooper
50 bottom	Harald Sund/TIB
51 top	Larry Geddis
51 bottom	Steve Solum
52	Larry Geddis
53	Tom & Pat Leeson
54 (2)	Harald Sund/TIB
56-57	Harald Sund/TIB
58	Ed Cooper
59	Ray Atkeson Photography
60-61	Ric Ergenbright
62 (2)	Harald Sund/TIB
63	Tom & Pat Leeson
64 (2)	Ed Cooper
65 (2)	Ed Cooper
66-67	Steve Satushek/TIB
68 top	Russell D. Lamb/Stockphotos, Inc.
68 bottom	Manuel Rodriguez/TIB
69 top	Harald Sund/TIB
69 bottom	Ed Cooper
70 (2)	Steve Solum
71	Tom & Pat Leeson
72 top	Harald Sund/TIB
72 bottom	Steve Satushek/TIB
73 (3)	Ed Cooper
74	Harald Sund/TIB
75	Harald Sund/TIB
76	Harald Sund/TIB
77 top left	Andrea Pistolesi/TIB
77 top right	Steve Solum
77 bottom	Ray Atkeson Photography
78 top left	Cliff Feulner/TIB
78 top right	Harald Sund/TIB
78 bottom	Andrea Pistolesi/TIB
79 top	C. Kuhn, Inc./TIB
79 center	Grant V. Faint/TIB
79 bottom	Steve Solum
80 top	Cliff Feulner/TIB
80 bottom	Andy Caulfield/TIB
81 top left	Allan Seiden/TIB
81 top right	Allan Seiden/TIB
81 bottom	Andrea Pistolesi/TIB
82 top left	Eddie Hironaka/TIB
82 top right	Nick Nicholson/TIB
82 center	Andy Caulfield/TIB
82 bottom	Richard Magruder/TIB
83 top	Cliff Feulner/TIB
83 bottom	Andrea Pistolesi/TIB
84 top left	Ed Cooper
84 top right	Ric Ergenbright
84 bottom	Ed Cooper
85 top left	Andrea Pistolesi/TIB
85 top right	Eddie Hironaka/TIB
85 bottom	Ed Cooper
86	Harald Sund/TIB
87 (2)	Ed Cooper
88-89	Harald Sund/TIB
90 (2)	Cindy McIntyre/Stockphotos, Inc.
91 top	Tom & Pat Leeson
91 bottom	Brett Froomer/TIB
92-93	Harald Sund/TIB
94 top	C. Kuhn, Inc./TIB
94 center	Tom & Pat Leeson
94 bottom	Cliff Fuelner/TIB
95	Ed Cooper
96 top	Tom & Pat Leeson
96 bottom	Joanne Pavia
97	Ric Ergenbright
98-99	Tom & Pat Leeson
100 (2)	Ed Cooper
101 top	Tom & Pat Leeson
101 bottom	Ed Cooper
102 top	Ed Cooper
102 bottom	Tom & Pat Leeson
103	Ed Cooper
104 (2)	Ed Cooper
106 top	Bullaty/Lomeo/TIB
106 bottom left	James H. Carmichael, Jr./TIB
106 bottom right	Ed Cooper
107 top	Grant V. Faint/TIB
107 bottom	Steve Satushek/TIB
108 top	Tom & Pat Leeson
108 bottom	Ed Cooper
109 top left	Gary Crallé/TIB
109 top right	Tom & Pat Leeson
109 bottom	Tom Mareschal/TIB
110 top left	David W. Hamilton/TIB
110 top right	Steve Satushek/TIB
110 bottom	Daniel Sikorskyi
111	Gary Crallé/TIB
112-113	Brett Froomer/TIB
114-115	Tom & Pat Leeson
116 (2)	Jürgen Vogt/TIB
117	Grant V. Faint/TIB
118 top	Grant V. Faint/TIB
118 bottom	Larry Dale Gordon/TIB
119	David Brownell/TIB
120	Grant V. Faint/TIB
121	Wes Bergen/Root Resources
122 top	Jürgen Vogt/TIB
122 center	Albert Normandin/TIB
122 bottom	Albert Normandin/TIB
123	Grant V. Faint/TIB
124 top	Jürgen Vogt/TIB
124 bottom	Tom & Pat Leeson
125 (2)	Grant V. Faint/TIB
126	Rob Atkins/TIB
127 top	Rob Atkins/TIB
127 bottom	Jürgen Vogt/TIB
128 top	Albert Normandin/TIB
128 center	Brett Froomer/TIB
128 bottom	Richard & Mary Magruder/TIB
129	Brett Froomer/TIB
130 top	Larry Dale Gordon/TIB
130 bottom	JaneArt Ltd./TIB
131 top	Jürgen Vogt/TIB
131 bottom	Harald Sund/TIB
132	John Lewis Stage/TIB
133 top	Brett Froomer/TIB
133 bottom	Larry Dale Gordon/TIB
134 top	P. von Baich/G J Images/TIB
134 bottom	Tom & Pat Leeson
135 top	Rob Atkins/TIB
135 bottom	Grant V. Faint/TIB
136 top	Peter Miller/TIB
136 bottom	Morton Beebe/TIB
137	Morton Beebe/TIB
138	Steve Satushek/TIB
139 (2)	Steve Satushek/TIB
140-141	Steve Satushek/TIB
142 top left	William A. Logan/TIB
142 top right	Ed Cooper
142 bottom	Ed Cooper
143	Ed Cooper
144 (2)	Pat O'Hara
145	Pat O'Hara
146-147	Pat O'Hara
148 (2)	Pat O'Hara
149 (2)	Pat O'Hara
150	Pat O'Hara
151 (3)	Pat O'Hara
152-153	Steve Satushek/TIB
154 top	Pat O'Hara
154 bottom	Steve Satushek/TIB
155	Steve Satushek/TIB
156-157	Pat O'Hara
158 (3)	Pat O'Hara
159	Grant V. Faint/TIB
160 top	Gary Crallé/TIB
160 bottom	Pat O'Hara
161	Pat O'Hara
162	Norman Clasen/TIB
163 (2)	Grafton Marshall Smith/TIB
164 top	Gary Crallé/TIB
164 bottom	Brett Froomer/TIB
165	Grant V. Faint/TIB
166-167	Grant V. Faint/TIB
168 (2)	Grant V. Faint/TIB
169	Tim Fitzharris
170 top left	Nick Nicholson/TIB
170 top right	Jay Freis/TIB
170 bottom	Nick Nicholson/TIB
172-173	Harald Sund/TIB
174 top	Brett Froomer/TIB
174 center	JaneArt Ltd./TIB
174 bottom	JaneArt Ltd./TIB
175 top	Steve Satushek/TIB
175 bottom	Ron Sanford/Black Star
176-177	Harald Sund/TIB
178 (2)	Ernest Manewal/Black Star
179	Ernest Manewal/Black Star
180	Ernest Manewal/Black Star
181	Flip Chalfant/TIB
182-183	Jake Rajs/TIB
184	Ernest Manewal/Black Star
185	Paul Slaughter/TIB
186 top	Jake Rajs/TIB
186 bottom	Brett Froomer/TIB
187	Ernest Manewal/Black Star
188-189	Harald Sund/TIB
190-191	Harald Sund/TIB